JUROR NUMBER FOUR

JUROR NUMBER FOUR

THE TRIAL OF THIRTEEN

BLACK PANTHERS AS SEEN FROM

THE JURY BOX

By Edwin Kennebeck

W · W · NORTON & COMPANY · INC ·

NEW YORK

Library of Congress Cataloging in Publication Data
Kennebeck, Edwin.
    Juror number four.
    1. Black Panthers Trial, New York, 1970–1971.
I. Title.
KF224.B55K4   345′.73′0231   72–10228
ISBN 0–393–08546–5

Printed in the United States of America.

1 2 3 4 5 6 7 8 9 0

For My Parents

"Unless we are put in touch—in life and literature—with the felt experiences of others, our own feelings atrophy. We need to be more than rationally *informed* about feeling; we need to *feel*—to respond directly with our own emotions to those of others."

MARTIN DUBERMAN, *The Uncompleted Past*

Contents

My appreciation to many people, including the copy-editing staff at Viking, for Carrying On—Nancy Guelich, Susan Mabon, Shirley Brownrigg, Georgette Felix, James Ricketson, Dorothy Seystahl—and to Teresa Egan, and all the others there who bore with my absences. To the defense lawyers and their assistant, Ruth Silber, for making their copy of the court transcript available and for general cooperation. To my friend James Tamulis, for criticism with encouragement. To John Anderson, for valuable help with proofs. To Don Erickson, for the right advice at the right time. To Carol Houck Smith, my editor. To my fellow jurors, for helping me with details, and for being among the best citizens.

In quoting from the Court transcript I have often omitted repetitious or irrelevant comments and have substituted ellipsis marks.

Present at the Trial

Jurors

INGRAM FOX. Composer, lecturer; black.

WILLIAM BEISER. History teacher; white.

STEPHEN CHABERSKI. Graduate student (political science); white.

EDWIN KENNEBECK. Editor; white.

FREDERICK HILLS. Editor; white.

NILS RASMUSSEN. Television film editor; white.

HIRAM IRIZARRY. Maintenance man; Puerto Rican.

ELETER YANES. Clerk, New York State Insurance Company; black.

BENJAMIN GILES. Retired longshoreman; black.

CHARLES BOWSER. Welfare Department supervisor; black.

JAMES BUTTERS. High-school teacher; white.

JOSEPH GARY. Post Office clerk; black.

Alternate Jurors

CLAUDETTE SULLIVAN. Finance officer; black.

JOSEPH RAINATO. Mechanical engineer; white.

OBIE TUNSTALL. Post Office clerk; black.

MURRAY SCHNEIDER. New York State Employment Service interviewer; white.

Defendants

AFENI SHAKUR (Alice Williams)
LUMUMBA SHAKUR (Anthony Coston)
MICHAEL TABOR (Cetewayo)
RICHARD MOORE (Analye Dharuba)
WALTER JOHNSON (Baba Odinga)
ALI BEY HASSAN (John Casson)
LEE ROPER (Shaba Om)
JOAN BIRD
ROBERT COLLIER
CURTIS POWELL
WILLIAM KING (Kwando Kinshasa)
ALEX MCKEIVER (Abayama Katara)
CLARK SQUIRE

Defense Attorneys

GERALD LEFCOURT   SANFORD KATZ
CAROL LEFCOURT   ROBERT BLOOM
WILLIAM CRAIN   CHARLES T. MCKINNEY

Prosecuting Attorneys

JOSEPH A. PHILLIPS   JEFFREY WEINSTEIN

Judge

JOHN M. MURTAGH

JUROR NUMBER FOUR

Ingram Fox et Al.

I worried about Ingram Fox. He was our jury foreman, acting too much like a man with Serious Civic
Responsibilities. An excellent, distinguished man, but reserved, stern, proper. Was he "fair"? Would I be able
to argue with him reasonably when we got to deliberations?

I didn't know much about the jury system, and
hadn't seriously asked myself whether I believed in it.
Suddenly I was on a jury for the first time in my mild
middle-aged life, which fact itself must have signaled
that I saw some usefulness in the process. Or was I just
curious about such a heavy trial? The defendants were
thirteen Black Panthers accused by New York State of
attempted murder, conspiracy to kill policemen, bomb
New York department stores, blow up subways and railroad tracks, and many other crimes, including my favor-
ites, "reckless endangerment" and "criminal mischief." If
we found them guilty, they could be jailed for the rest of
their lives.

Black Panthers! These were the famous men and
women held on $100,000 bail—later reduced somewhat
for a few—who were originally known as the Panther 21.

By the time they came to trial, eight of the names on the indictment were gone—a couple of the defendants could not be found, others were held elsewhere on different charges, or had been severed from the case because they were ill or too young. They were ghetto blacks for whom a party had been given at the Leonard Bernsteins' apartment to raise defense money. Tom Wolfe, the gifted irritator, had written his Radical Chic article about it.

Kingman Brewster of Yale had said that it was impossible for a black man to get a fair trial in this country. But here we were in the Criminal Court Building at 100 Centre Street, Manhattan, in the autumn of 1970, giving it a try—twelve jurors with four alternates, a motley crew, neither radical nor chic, a New York assemblage sitting in our allotted chairs in two legal rows in our legal box; a white-haired Judge at the bench, above it all (not really); a stocky affable State Assistant District Attorney laying on us a parade of witnesses and armfuls of evidence; and the defendants, eleven men and two women, sitting across the room at their L-shaped table, with another L of six young lawyers in front of them—all in a large courtroom bustling with dozens of guards, rows of spectators, and two tables of reporters: the justice machine, and me, by some fluke, a cog therein. *People of the State of New York* v. *Lumumba Shakur et al.*

I can't define "fair trial." For one thing it includes the assurance of good lawyers on both sides, and blacks have so many charges against whites that I find it almost frivolous to try a definition. But as the DA gives us the broad, dismaying outlines of his case, telling us about the dynamite that one secret agent discovered, and as he brings into the courtroom guns and bullets, books on explosives, and witnesses who participated in the Panthers' talk of violent revolution, I am hit hard by the possibility that something may indeed have gotten out of hand a couple of years before among those angry blacks. We're sitting in the jury box, passing rifles and shotguns and automatics to each other. I'm holding a cumbersome M-14, trying to lift and examine the heavy gun without knocking fellow jurymen Fred Hills at my left or Steve Chaberski at my right, while the spectators— some of them wives or parents of the defendants—probably wonder what this small arsenal signifies to me and the other jurors.

The M-14 belonged to Michael Tabor (Ta-*bor*), the DA says. It was lying on Tabor's bed when the arresting officers came to his apartment; they also say they found two shotguns, a pistol, and a pair of handcuffs. Now I am holding a clip of shells that came with the rifle; they're like the ones I handled in air force gunnery training during World War II. Now—another rainy morning or drawn-out warm afternoon—I am inspecting a can labeled "Gunpowder," supposedly found in another Panther apartment, turning it in my hand to study the label or sniff inside, then passing it to Fred. Later a black undercover detective on the witness stand is telling us some of the things he heard the Panthers saying—how they would kidnap a "pig" and hold him for ransom, or kill one, or place bombs on the New Haven Railroad tracks, or try out a Molotov cocktail in some park, rehearsing for the insurrection.

I didn't like the idea of blowing up Manhattan or any part thereof. I could say that I would follow my conscience and, despite misgivings about the other jurors, I knew that they would do likewise. Six blacks, five whites, one Puerto Rican; only one was a woman, black. We had four alternate jurors, a black woman, a black man, and two white men. There was no hanky-panky to be suspected among any of the sixteen, no special pleading or blind-spot groping. I didn't doubt that Mr. Fox would follow his conscience; I just didn't know how that conscience had been formed in this prosperous-looking black man, "where it was coming from."

Panthers brazenly yelled their slogans about power and freedom while they brandished guns and revolutionary slogans, and the charges against these particular Panthers were severe. With no idea how the trial would progress, I imagined myself trying to win Foreman Fox to my viewpoint on some grave question of conspiratorial guilt. Such a complicated case was bound to raise hundreds of arguable points—wasn't it?

Ingram Fox was a bald, middle-aged black man who seemed to have the biggest smile at 100 Centre Street (the second biggest smile belonged to William Beiser, the tall white juror who sat next to him). Mr. Fox, composer, was born in Guiana, and his voice had the lilt of the Caribbean. He had been scheduled to go to Germany in October 1970 for a production of his opera *Dan Fodio* (the name of a real Nigerian leader); instead, he had chosen to take a role in this other dramatic spectacle. His smile didn't conceal his profoundly stern demeanor. He dressed so well, so conservatively, that I could imagine the Panthers calling him Uncle Tom; yet they had taken him on their jury.

I didn't know much about Fox. He and Beiser had already been seated in the first two jury seats when I came into the courtroom as part of a panel of forty-two New Yorkers in mid-September 1970. As I sat in one of the spectator seats with my fellow citizens—like parishioners in varnished pews—I thought that those two jurors seemed lonely and a little comic up there. I hadn't heard the long interrogation they had gone through, individually, sitting in the witness box. But because I was the fourth juror to make the grade, and the original number-three man was excused because of ill health, I sat through the interrogation—the voir dire— of all the others, and learned a little about their attitudes on blacks, police, revolution. As the trial dragged on— it went from October 1970 to May 1971—I wondered how many of these jurors could sort out charges against the Panthers objectively—i.e., *my* way.

I let myself develop suspicions about Ingram Fox from the thinnest of observations. One day, a few weeks into the trial, Assistant District Attorney Joseph Phillips was getting ready to show us Gillo Pontecorvo's film *The Battle of Algiers,* which he believed had served as revolutionary inspiration for the defendants. After we filed into the first two rows of the spectator section for this event, Judge John M. Murtagh asked the foreman whether his jury could see the small screen well enough. My impression was that Mr. Fox hastily said, "Yes, Your Honor," *then* looked around to check. Aha! And a few weeks later, in the jury room during a recess, Mr. Fox scolded me because one of the Court officers had brought him a note I had written to the Judge, asking about some bit of evidence. Some of the other jurors joined in the teapot tempest. I wondered why the Court officer had not taken up the matter with me, but I saw that I had made a mistake—should have sent the note through the foreman, but didn't because I was afraid he would be unwilling to "bother" the Judge. I apologized to Mr. Fox, and realized that if the question were important enough the lawyers would probably think of it. (It wasn't.)

But the way Fox had pounced on me was unsettling. Would this formidable black man be fair and reasonable? I didn't think of asking myself whether *I* would. And I only half-thought that he might be worrying about me, the upstart.

My fourteen other jury colleagues were also cheerfully enigmatic, and various. From such Walks of Life! Postal clerks, two. New York State employees, the two women and one man. Editors, two (I was one). A supervisor from the City Welfare Department. An apartment-building maintenance man. A man who edited television documentary films. A graduate student in political science. A retired longshoreman. Et al.—mem-

bers of the System, nobody starving. The six black jurors, who were at least comfortably off, did not seem
inclined toward revolutionary sympathies. The Puerto
Rican maintenance man had said at the voir dire that he
was not aware of racial discrimination in New York
City. The whites seemed to range from intensely liberal
to cautiously mainstream. We couldn't know each other
very well in the first few weeks. We couldn't really
know each other until the final hours of the trial.

The DA's case was perturbing. From the court
transcript, as the Judge read the main portions of the
indictment:

"The defendants, in the County of New York, from
on or about August 1, 1968, continually to on or about
April 2, 1969, with the intent to engage in conduct
constituting the crime of murder, agreed among themselves and with others to engage in and cause the performance of conduct constituting the crime of murder."

Not murder but conspiracy to commit murder; not
killing but agreeing to kill.

"During the course of the conspiracy, the defendants were members of the Black Panther Party, which
utilized a para-military [on three different occasions His
Honor said "parimutuel," then corrected it] structure
and discipline in the pursuit of its objectives. . . . The
members of this party were required to wear uniforms
and carry weapons. . . . Lumumba Abdul Shakur was
the captain of the New York City area and a member
of the central staff of the Black Panther Party. William

King was a lieutenant for security. . . . Richard Moore was a field marshal for the New York area and a member of the central staff. Michael Tabor was a captain for security for New York State and Clark Squires [Squire] was a lieutenant for finance in New York City. Robert Collier was minister of education. . . . Afeni Shakur and Larry Mack [he was not present at the trial] were the section leaders of the Black Panther Party, part of an over-all plan to harass and destroy those elements of society which the defendants regarded as part of the power structure.

"The defendants agreed to assassinate police officers by means of bombs and guns. . . . As part of said conspiracy, the defendants planned coordinated bombings of the 24th Police Precinct, the 44th Police Precinct, and Queens Branch of the Board of Education with dynamite. . . ."

Those bombing plans were for January 1969; and for Easter of that year the defendants were supposed to have agreed to bomb another precinct station "on or about April 3, 1969. With respect to this bombing it was agreed that while the police were investigating the station house explosion, the defendants would detonate six bombs on predetermined sites along the New Haven Railroad's tracks. It was also the plan of the defendants that the attacks on the precinct and the railroad line would be coordinated with the bombing of a number of department stores during the Easter shopping season."

Then, said the Judge, "the indictment proceeds to list some 29 overt acts, acts allegedly committed in furtherance of the conspiracy. . . . The additional counts in the indictment charge the defendants with the crimes of attempted murder, conspiracy in the second degree, an attempt to commit arson in the first degree, the crime of arson in the first degree, the crime of arson in the second degree, the crime of conspiracy in the third degree, the crime of criminal mischief in the third degree, and the crime of possessing a weapon, dangerous instrument and appliance."

Judge Murtagh gave his own explanation of conspiracy in terms that seemed clear enough but must have lodged in all our minds with annoying persistence. Conspiracy, a crime with dangerously murky definitions: "It is exactly like what we see in a play. [Surprising that someone trained in legal precision should say "exactly" when no metaphor is perfect.] We have actors with roles of varying importance. Some have major parts. Some have minor parts. But all of them are players. It is not necessary to be a player, that a person be the leading man or that he play an important role. If his or her part requires him or her to do no more than walk across the stage, or calls for the utterance of but a single sentence, he or she is a player, despite the unimportance of his or her role." No problem here about top billing.

"The court estimates that the trial may last for a period of three months. The period will be longer if counsel for the respective parties do not present the evidence expeditiously or other factors intervene. . . ."

Most of us heard the principal charges read several

times, because the voir dire kept using up the panels—
the groups of prospective jurors who were chosen by
lot down at 60 Centre Street and sent up to 100, to the
lucky thirteenth floor. The DA or his young assistant
Jeffrey Weinstein, and various combinations of defense
lawyers with Afeni Shakur and Michael Tabor (Cetewayo)—who were defending themselves—questioned
maybe a dozen citizens a day about backgrounds and
prejudices, about their confidence that they could be fair.
One prospect after another didn't think he or she could
evaluate the evidence objectively, or could stay away
from a job for a long time, or could take the strain of
such a serious trial. Or else the prosecution or defense,
deciding that a man or woman was prejudiced, exercised
a peremptory challenge. Each side was allowed twenty
of these. Just before each panel was used up another
group arrived, and Judge Murtagh again read the major
points of the indictment, so they would know what they
were in for.

As the days passed, we tried to become familiar
with the faces of the defendants, their varying degrees
of black, various ages, various attitudes; the alleged criminals. "Juror, look upon the defendants. Defendants,
look upon the juror," the clerk had intoned as I was
sworn in on September 24, 1970. Ceremony. Living
theater. The defendants stood up during this solemn
moment. Afeni Shakur, at the nearest end of their table,
her young face a study in African beauty and Harlem
hauteur, lounged against the table, bored, chewing gum,
and looked upon me. Next, her husband Lumumba

Shakur; then Michael Tabor, a tall, husky athlete; then Richard Moore (Dharuba), almond eyes flashing in the dark face past a Levantine nose.

But it wasn't easy to sort them out by name, even after looking over at them during the six-week voir dire. On the second day of the actual trial, I said to Fred Hills, "Maybe we should ask the Judge to have the defendants all introduced." Fred thought it was a good idea, and it happened that another juror, Jim Butters, had made the same suggestion to Ingram Fox. So we talked about it in the jury room during a recess and then sent a note to the Judge. In the courtroom he had the lawyers ask their clients to rise, one by one, as their names were called. Most of them gave a restrained clenched-fist salute.

There was no consistency about identification during the trial, so we got to know some of the Panthers by their resonant, astonishing African names and others by their original ordinary "slave names." After Richard Moore came Baba Odinga, also known as (a.k.a.) Walter Johnson. Ali Bey Hassan. Shaba Om, a.k.a. Lee Roper. Joan Bird, whose face I could barely see because she sat at the corner of the table, partially hidden behind Roper. She was nineteen years old when she was arrested. Robert Collier, light-skinned, whose thin droopy mustache gave him a mandarin look—like a captive prince, as Murray Kempton wrote later. Curtis Powell. William King (Kinshasa). Alex McKeiver (Katara), also light-skinned and also young. Finally Clark Squire, who wore shades and seemed sullen. They often talked to each other and laughed and passed notes.

It didn't take long to register reactions to the young defense lawyers. Somehow each one of them seemed to be programmed to a choice adjective. The leader, insofar as there was a leader, seemed to be Gerald Lefcourt; the description "wiry" hung over him like a blurb in a cartoon. Sitting in front of Afeni Shakur, he was the most visible—a dynamic short man with a smashing Afro-style head of hair (he's white) and wide sideburns. His sister-in-law, Carol Lefcourt, sat next to him, a pretty, "petite," unemphatic, shrewd young woman. William Crain, his hair long in back, was balding and wore a goatee and, being impulsive, "impish," was probably Judge Murtagh's most nettlesome bother.

Sanford Katz, also with a prematurely high forehead, with horn-rimmed glasses, long brown hair in back, whom the Judge correctly called "sarcastic" many times —as if the word were legally pejorative—stung like a wasp in his outbursts against witnesses, the DA, the Judge, the whole justice machine as it was being revved up in that courtroom; "This is not a Victorian tea party," he explained to one and all after an admonition from the bench. Robert Bloom, relaxed and "bearlike," had a deceptively gentle manner. He tended to smile, smile, and sometimes my facial mechanisms were strained by a determination not to respond despite the urge to. Bloom: "May I be heard on that, Your Honor?" The Court: "No need to." Bloom: "Your Honor, I feel a need to."

The sixth and last was the only black attorney,

Charles T. McKinney. "Courtly." He knew all the rules well and followed them, his elegant dark face and gentle tone capable of easing a nervous prospective woman juror into admitting—after an hour or so of questions— that no, actually she didn't think she wanted to serve on this trial.

Looking at the defendants gave me no clues, of course, to their guilt or innocence. Judge Murtagh kept repeating the edifying/disturbing American principle that the defendants are "presumed innocent until proven guilty," and most of us are willing to go along with that although it doesn't mean what it says (neither does "In God We Trust" on the wall over the Judge's head). It's a tautly phrased formula, the kind we need to function by, I suppose. But if the defendants were really pre- sumed innocent, why were any of them kept in jail? Nine of the thirteen were still locked up, had been for a year and a half, because their bail was so high—now $25,000 to $100,000. And *"until* proven guilty," if you want to be persnickety (I am a book editor, persnickety from birth), seems to imply that they will be proven guilty. A better phrasing—but try to stomach it—would be "Neither innocent nor guilty unless and until proven guilty."

There was no question of their having to be proven innocent. That is one of the beautiful wild claims that the American system makes. As the defense lawyers kept reminding us during the voir dire, the Perry Mason ex- pectation that the accused will produce alibis and proofs of pure guiltlessness doesn't legally apply in U.S. real

life. It was the full burden of the DA to validate his and
the grand jury's charges. There were lots of them—
thirty counts in the complete indictment—and the defense lawyers had their hands full.

According to the DA—"We will try to show that
the defendants are a small group of fanatics"—New
York City would have had a wild and tragic Easter week
in 1969, if the police force hadn't sent gangs of their
men, heavily armed and wearing bulletproof vests, to
arrest the Panthers in their various apartments at 5:00
A.M. on April 2, a Wednesday. Ladies' handbags for sale
in Bloomingdale's and Macy's and Alexander's would
have been loaded with bombs to blast the innocent shop-
pers. Subway and railroad tracks would have been blown
up by dynamite and Molotov cocktails and pieces of
plumbing pipe packed with gunpowder.

In fact, according to the DA, as early as January
1969 the school building and two police stations mentioned in the indictment just missed being blown up because police spy Ralph White replaced the Panthers'
dynamite with fake sticks concocted in the Bomb Squad
laboratories. Some chemical experts mixed up a batch of
clay, oatmeal, and stuff that would glow under an ultraviolet light, rolled it into "sticks," and put it in the dynamite wrappers. Since White later saw some of the Panthers passing those sticks around, and the debris from
aborted explosions was to shine before our eyes under
the special lamp, the DA would prove to us that the defendants had tried to carry out a mini-revolution three
months before their Easter celebrations.

Despite all that, in those first days of the trial I was able to gaze at the defendants without getting fanatic vibrations from them. Afeni Shakur's contemptuous manner erupted now and then as she questioned a prospect, or commented to His Honor on the proceedings, but I was almost as amused, or interested, as I was disturbed. Occasionally Michael Tabor, in his deep cello voice, got off some fiery remarks about the Constitution. Once he stood up to complain about the defendants' lunch, and a member of the group held up one of the sandwiches they had been given. A mouse dropped to the floor and ran up the aisle, a woman shrieked, and the unperturbed Judge continued with the trial. Later, both Afeni and Lumumba Shakur would hiss "Sit down, sit down!" as DA Phillips made some objection.

Mr. Phillips usually took this without comment, but one day Afeni Shakur leaned her head back and softly sang "Your Cheatin' Heart," which goaded him into a complaint. Another time, when Mr. Phillips interrupted with some patently improper remark, she stood up and exclaimed, "I object, I ob-*ject*, *I ob-ject!*" And on another occasion, when the Judge banged his hand down to protest some interruption (he didn't use a gavel), the defendants pounded their table in antiphon. I made an effort not to frown and not to smile. Likewise one afternoon, when His Honor said he would dismiss us a little early because he had to meet with some other judges upstairs, and one of the defendants said, "Oh, wow."

I wasn't going to navigate by "vibrations" anyway; but maybe my liberal conscience was too eager to excuse them as victims of society. Was my sense of white middle-class guilt about to be tested severely?

The Judge's comportment during these flurries was surprisingly lenient, no doubt by deliberate plan, perhaps suggested from higher levels in order to avoid the nasty cul-de-sac that Judge Julius Hoffman had stumbled into during the Chicago conspiracy trial. I suspected that Manhattan District Attorney Frank Hogan might have privately expressed the hope that no Bobby Seales would be bound and gagged this time.

I began to wonder, like a good liberal, whether Judge Murtagh—white of hair, firm of voice—was the ideal disinterested party. An amateur juror like myself, even in such a long trial, finds it difficult to sort out the technicalities of the law, but I nurtured a suspicion that His Honor, consciously or not, might be infected by the prejudices—against some blacks, against young revolutionaries, against the threat of change—that seem to afflict most elder whites. His Honor gave no indication, as far as I could tell, that he thought the thirteen Panthers might be justly angered.

But the majesty of the stern man in black robes, wearing horn-rimmed glasses, in his comfortable chair behind the bench, with his chrome carafe of water (the other participants had bright plastic pitchers) and his seasoned authority over guards and clerks and assistants —the awesome and austere power that the Judge represented made me feel old-fashioned respect, which I didn't shake off during the whole trial.

"To Speak the Truth"

Voir dire: Norman French term meaning "to speak the truth." A system by which attorneys of both sides question people directly, under the guidance of the Judge. A beautiful way to build a jury, the fairest of them all. It was a clear opportunity to watch fate at work.

I don't know what angel of cool had been in charge that September day in 1970 when the Court clerk summoned me to the witness chair. As I look through the transcript now I am surprised at my laconic responses: Maybe I was too nervous to be anything but terse. I had always hated to face audiences, and ordinarily I would have been further discomposed by the microphone I had to speak at.

"Mr. Kennebeck, sir"—Mr. Phillips, respectful and efficient, began with his usual questions—"have you been able to hear us this morning, this afternoon, and on the prior day you were here?"

"For the most part, yes," I said.

"And have we said anything so far that gives you any doubt about your ability to serve fairly and impartially in this particular case?"

"No."

"And is there any observation you would like to make about what we have said up until now before we start?"

"I don't believe so."

"Can you tell me, sir, how long you are with your present organization?"

"Fifteen years."

"And is that some type of publishing organization?"

"Yes, sir."

"What organization?"

"The Viking Press."

"And can you tell me in what phase of their operation you are involved?"

"I am in charge of the copy-editing department for senior books."

"Can you tell me what type of books you deal with mainly, sir? It's a very poor question, I know, but do your best to answer it."

Actually, the question wasn't poor at all. "It's a great variety, from picture, art books to history and novels and social commentary."

Mr. Phillips asked me whether I had been on jury duty before; I said I had, but had never gotten further than this point.

"Now you hope to go further?" he said.

"Yes."

I wonder what that "Yes" of mine meant; I can't tabulate its significances—from ego-tripping to guilt to a sense of public service. But "Yes" was all I needed to say.

"Sir, I meant that humorously, but I do hope so—"

I said, "I think it would be very interesting to serve on this jury."

He asked whether I knew anything about conspiracy, arson, murder, and I said "No," then sagely added, "Nothing special." He asked a little about my background, and I told him I had been in the air force during World War II. I was a radio operator and gunner on a B-17 late in the war, but during bombing missions over Germany I never had to use guns. Not many of those details came through in my answer. I told him I was born in Colorado, went to college in Milwaukee, was single, didn't know much about this case, had no opinions on the guilt or innocence of the defendants, had no fixed opinion on the Black Panther Party, agreed that police brutality and racial injustice should be eliminated.

Then came a couple of questions based maybe on what might have seemed my benign, compassionate visage (really a mask over a bundle of perplexities): "If you felt, sir, that someone believed in a cause and therefore did some actions that were illegal as a result of that, would you think that would absolve them from wrongdoing?"

I must have gone into a meditation. Phillips said, "Do you follow my question, sir?"

Still meditating.

"You've heard of Robin Hood, I take it?"

"Yes," I said.

"And you've heard of robbing from the rich to give to the poor?"

"Yes." Now what? I hate to lose games and quizzes, but maybe this would be my downfall.

"But nevertheless it's robbery," Phillips said. "You understand that, don't you?"

"Well, yes, I understand that."

Here Judge Murtagh intervened, to my surprise and gratitude: "Please ask a proper question."

The DA went on. "I may have one more question in that area and I'll go on to something else. Do you have any reservations in your mind that if Robin Hood were indicted for robbery, that you would convict him of robbery even though he might have wanted to give the money to the poor?"

Gawd. I meditated. "I'd have to hear the evidence—the answer is no." Meaning that I didn't have any reservations. But who can really answer questions like that?

The Judge said, "Mr. District Attorney, get along with it. Please do not prolong the questioning."

Mr. Phillips asked an even more speculative and difficult question. "Sir, I'm going to conclude. I just have a couple of other questions and they relate to the last question I've asked each of the prior jurors and the ones you've probably heard today, and they go to, essentially, your ability to serve, when the case goes to verdict—in other words, if you were in the jury room and the vote was eleven to one and you were the only minority juror, would you continue to reason with the rest of your fellow jurors to try to reach a result or would you just say, 'I've made up my mind. I'm brighter than the rest of you fellows and let's not discuss it'?"

Inasmuch as nine of the jury places were still empty, and I had not met the three men already seated, I couldn't imagine whom I would be dealing with on that far-off day. I certainly didn't consider myself brighter than the present and future jurors. Anyhow, the DA's phrasing of his questions practically dictated the answer. "No, I would continue to reason with them."

The DA alluded again indirectly to my college education. "And just because someone didn't have the same experience and background that you might have, but might have some common sense, would you also listen to that type of person?"

"Certainly."

When Mr. Phillips finished with me, it was late afternoon, and we recessed for the day. I had a curious evening of suspension; I went to dinner with friends, who agreed that I wouldn't get on the jury. "The prosecution never wants liberal editorial types."

In the morning I resumed the place of honor so the defense could evaluate my credentials.

Mr. Lefcourt asked me what college I had attended. Marquette University in Milwaukee. Did I have brothers and sisters? Yes; one was in the army, probably not likely to be shipped to Vietnam at that point. Would I have any problem if I knew that the defendants were opposed to the Vietnam war? Good God, no. But I only said, "No."

"I assume that you have heard a great deal about the Black Panther Party?"

"Yes. . . ."

"Is there anything in your reading which caused an opinion to form in your mind which may be a problem here on this trial?"

"No."

"You feel you could be fair and open?"

"Yes. . . ."

"Would the fact that there are undercover agents in the case prejudice you in any way against the defendants?"

"I don't believe so."

"And is it fair to say that you wouldn't take the word of an undercover agent over that of anybody else?"

"Yes, that's fair. . . ."

"Should you be selected for the jury in this case, and there comes a time when you are in deliberation, is it fair to say that if you have arrived at a decision which you believe is based on the evidence, that you will not be pressured into changing your view merely because you might be in the minority?"

Oh, I'll take on those three strangers and the empty chairs! "I think that's fair to say."

"And that would be true even if you were a single holdout?"

"Yes."

"And therefore could never reach a verdict by the jury?"

"I wouldn't change my mind just for the sake of unanimity."

"Thank you very much. I have no further questions."

Charles McKinney, black attorney, came over. Mr. McKinney of the courtly diction. "Mr. Kennebeck, it is an inescapable fact that in this case each of the defendants is a black man and naturally there is concern that that fact should not enter into the judgment of any prospective juror, recognizing the fact that all of us harbor some kind of prejudice, but it's a question as to what extent you are able to suppress it. Do you feel, sir, that you might in any way, conscious or unconscious, be affected by some prejudice or bias that might interfere with your passing judgment upon thirteen black men and women who are charged with a serious crime?"

"No, I don't believe so."

From such answers, how could they know what sort of person I was? McKinney kept probing, maybe for some word or intonation that would give him a deeper clue.

I had mentioned earlier, in answer to a question about run-ins with the police, that my apartment had been burglarized some years before. McKinney said, "Is there anything about the fact that you have been the victim of a crime, that, perhaps unknowingly, might affect you in passing judgment upon thirteen men and women who are accused of a crime or crimes?"

"No, because I don't know who committed the crime." I should have added that it wouldn't have made any difference if I had known.

McKinney, too, wondered about the effect of my educational accomplishments. (I still can't give Henry V's dates, or even George Washington's.) "Do you feel that as a result of your educational background and as a result of your experience and perhaps somewhat being removed from some areas of life, that you would have difficulty in passing judgment upon thirteen men and women, some of whom have not been so fortunate as to receive as much education or to experience some of the experiences that you have had?"

I had admired many aspects of the Black Panther Party, I sensed that much of their frightening talk was a form of self-respect. I wasn't going to let anyone's disadvantages, ignorance, poverty, turn me against them. But I didn't have to answer the question.

Mr. Phillips: "Objection."

The Court: "Sustained."

After two more questions about my fairness, McKinney said, "No further questions."

Mr. Phillips said that I was "acceptable to the People."

The defendants and their attorneys conferred quietly for a brief moment. Then William Crain said, "Your Honor, the juror is acceptable." The Judge said, "The juror will be sworn." I walked over to jury seat number four in some amazement, put my hand on the Bible, and proceeded to look upon the defendants.

"Who Chased Who?"
"I Chased You"

The Great Conspiracy had come to an end on the morning of Wednesday, April 2, 1969, and the arrested Panthers learned who had been spying on them. Some of my cojurors, no doubt, had seen District Attorney Frank Hogan on television later that day, appearing on news broadcasts in person—a rare gesture for him —to tell New Yorkers that they had just been saved from a day of slaughter. I hadn't seen the broadcast, but I've since looked up the *New York Times* account—on the front page:

> The Black Panthers, Mr. Hogan said, planned to plant bombs today in the midtown stores of Macy's, Alexander's, Bloomingdale's, Korvette's and Abercrombie and Fitch at the height of the Easter season shopping [sic]. . . .
>
> The conspirators, Mr. Hogan said, planned to dynamite the tracks of the New Haven branch of the Penn Central at six points north of 148th Street. . . . "They agreed to assassinate police officers by bombs and guns and planned a number of other coordinated acts of violence," Mr. Hogan said.

The police also said they had confiscated three home-made pipe bombs.

Those arrests, of course, were the final chapter of the conspiracy, but Mr. Phillips presented them to us at the opening of the trial. The first witness we heard from was a policeman, a short man with a pleasant face of black granite. He was Sergeant George Abraham, who had arrested Richard Moore. That opening scene could not have been more antidramatic, with the policeman quietly walking up to the witness stand to be sworn in, and with the legal-formal roundabout questions carefully worded by the DA.

"Sergeant Abraham, did you have an assignment on the morning of April second, 1969?"

"Yes sir."

"What was that assignment?"

So it began. Some of the legal formulas led to further strange colloquies, easing our concentration a little. All the items of evidence had to be numbered and registered by the court clerks—a tedious process. A certain pistol and its bullets and holster became, for example, exhibits 37A, 37B, and 37C. When the DA asked an arresting detective what condition these exhibits were in when he found them, he said, "B was in A and A was in C." The jurors were all grateful for the chance to smile along with everyone else.

The policemen who appeared before us in the next couple of weeks left me with a collage-panorama of simultaneous knockings-on-doors in several parts of Manhattan and the Bronx. For me the picture cohered around the courtroom confrontation that we watched on October 26 and 27 between Michael Tabor and the man who had arrested him, Detective Joseph Coffey. The two men talked to each other with icy irony. Coffey, a good-looking, dark-haired white policeman of hefty build, may have been a little overweight but seemed to have great physical strength in addition to his power ex officio. Tabor, the tall athlete who seemed to loom over us as he stood near the jury box, had physical strength, even glamour, although *his* official status was low.

One of Tabor's first questions, spoken in a rich drawl, followed the phrasing of courtroom formula: "Is it not a fact, Detective Coffey, that the testimony you gave upon direct examination by the District Attorney yesterday as to how you arrested me was a deliberate lie?"

"Mr. Tabor," said the hearty detective, "you above everyone should know that it was the truth."

Coffey had already told us the main details of the arrest, but Tabor went over them and drew out more particulars. He asked the detective about his assignment on that busy morning, and Coffey said that at 3:00 A.M. he reported to the office of the DA's Office Squad and met about 150 other officers. This was in the same building where our trial was taking place. They were all briefed by Inspector William Knapp * of the Bureau of Special Services.

* Not to be confused with Whitman Knapp of the police corruption investigations that came to light in 1971.

"There were a hundred and fifty officers there?" asked Tabor—not merely for clarification, I would guess.

"Approximately, sir," said Coffey.

The politesse decorating the entire exchange, the addressings as "sir" and "detective," were like the wrong frame around a painting.

"During the course of that briefing, do you recall Inspector Knapp saying that several of the human beings who you were supposed to arrest would never be taken alive by pig police?"

"Yes, sir, you were one of them."

"Did Inspector Knapp also say that we were dangerous?"

"Extremely dangerous. . . ."

"The officers who were designated to carry out the Gestapo raids that night, were they equipped with any additional equipment other than their—"

The DA did not object, but the Judge spoke to Coffey: "You need not answer that question until it is put in proper form."

So Tabor censored the offending word: "The officers who were designated to carry out the predawn raids that morning, did they have additional equipment other than the type they normally carry?"

Besides the usual revolver, one man had a shotgun and they all had bulletproof vests, but Coffey didn't put his on because it was too small. The policemen left the DA's office about 4:30 A.M., drove to Harlem, and waited in Tabor's building until exactly 5:00. Tabor asked what they talked about as they drove uptown. Coffey: "As I remember it, it was mainly apprehension."

At the appointed hour, a black patrolman who was part of the team knocked on the apartment door, told the woman inside that there had been a complaint of noise, and asked her to let him in. She refused.

"Was there an actual noise complaint in that apartment?" Tabor said.

"No, sir."

"Then he was lying; is that correct? . . ."

"Yes, sir."

"He was lying. To your knowledge, is it a custom for police to lie whenever it is convenient for them?"

"The end justifies the means," said Coffey.

His black police colleague told the woman he had to have his memo book signed and it was too large to slip under the door.

Tabor said, "Have you ever lied to an occupant of an apartment by using the memo-book story?"

"I've used subterfuge, yes sir," Coffey said.

"You've lied?"

"Subterfuge."

"You told an untruth?"

"You call it what you want, sir."

At about the same time that morning, farther uptown in Manhattan, Police Sergeant George Abraham and four others were using subterfuge at the door of Richard Moore's apartment. Abraham was one of many policemen who appeared in the first weeks of the trial to describe this part of the story. He said he knocked on the door and told a woman inside that he was from the Welfare Department. She told him to come back later, it was too early. Abraham announced that he had an arrest warrant; the woman opened the door slightly and the cops pushed in, grabbed Moore, and handcuffed him.

At the Shakurs' apartment, also in Harlem, on West 117th Street, the subterfuge was an oily rag that the police burned outside the door, yelling that there was a fire in the building. Where there's smoke there's fire. The Shakurs opened the door. At Alex McKeiver's building on West 135th Street, one of the policemen, after they failed to get a response to their knocking, went downstairs and called on the intercom; he talked to McKeiver's young woman companion, whom he knew. He told her he wanted to talk to her, so when he came back up she opened the door for him, and all the cops went in.

Walter Johnson lived in Harlem too. The cops didn't get a response when they knocked; one of the team, who had been on an adjoining roof, told us he saw a leg emerging from a rear window of the apartment; he called out that he would shoot if whoever it was emerged any further, so the culprit went back inside; the cops were let in and they arrested Johnson.

Robert Collier lived on the Lower East Side; his door was opened at the police knock. Dr. Curtis Powell, who lived in the same neighborhood, wasn't at home when the cops arrived, so they broke in. They said they found the television set turned on. Near the end of the trial, when the defense put up a few witnesses, we learned that Powell came back to his apartment in the afternoon to be arrested. The police were still there, and had apparently somewhat messed up the premises, as we saw from photographs taken by a young white woman who was with Powell.

At Ali Bey Hassan's apartment in the Bronx the police were let in.

Detective Coffey told us that the noise complaint ruse at Tabor's apartment didn't work; the leader of the team, a Lieutenant Deutsch, said through the door, "I'm a police officer and I have a warrant for the arrest of Michael Tabor. Please open the door."

They waited a few seconds and got no response, so Deutsch ordered them to kick the door in.

Tabor said, "And upon being ordered by Lieutenant Deutsch to kick the door in, what did you do?"

"I kicked it in, sir."

"You carry out orders, is that correct?"

"Most definitely, sir."

"I'm sure you do," said Tabor, with no objection from DA or Judge.

"How many officers engaged in the door-kicking adventure?"

"More than one, sir. . . ."

"Did you partake?"

"Yes, sir."

"Did you enjoy it?"

"Not particularly, sir."

Coffey said that when the door opened, he was the first to enter. "At the end of the foyer I observed you and a young lady. . . ."

"And what was I doing when you observed us?"

"When I first saw you, you were standing there. . . ."

"Tell me, Detective Coffey, did you have your gun drawn at the time?"

"Yes, sir."

"Did your fellow officers have their guns drawn at the time?"

"Yes, sir."

Tabor asked about the man with the shotgun.

Coffey said, "The officer who had the shotgun, his knees locked, because he was down in a crouched position for over ten minutes, and he wasn't able to get into the apartment with the rest of us, sir. He came in last."

"The detective who had the shotgun got his *knees locked*"—Tabor caressed that phrase—"from the crouching position?"

The spectators were amused, and His Honor said, "I'll admonish this audience that I will clear this court-room if there is any repetition of laughter." I was sort of chewing my teeth to remind myself that it all wasn't funny.

"Was he very old?" asked Tabor.

"He's in his late forties," said Coffey. "He's also very sick, sir."

Tabor, wheeling a little as he tended to do during

his questioning, said, "Oh, that's unfortunate." He waited a moment. "Uh, is it normal to send an *old officer*, who is subject to catching *locked knees*, on such a dangerous mission?"

Assistant DA Weinstein objected and His Honor sustained, while I held my face in position.

"Would it be correct to say," Tabor asked, "that a chase ensued at that time?"

"A small chase, yes, sir."

"Who chased who?"

"I chased you, sir."

The Judge broke in. "Counselor Lefcourt, I want the record to reflect that throughout this testimony you have been giggling and laughing."

Tabor strode over to the defense table to ask Counselor Crain something as Lefcourt rose and said, "Quite frankly, I thought some of the questioning was quite funny, but I see no crime in laughing, Your Honor."

"That is not the first time," said the Judge. "It has been throughout this testimony, and you are in contempt of court."

"Well, Your Honor . . . I didn't realize that laughter was prohibited."

"I state for the record that you are in contempt of court. Be seated."

Lefcourt shook his head and grinned. "For laughing, Your Honor? For laughing?"

"Yes. And you will be seated."

Richard Moore joined in from the defendants' table: "You can only laugh when the Court laughs, when he finds something funny. What you should do is wear a mask."

The Judge didn't make any response to this. I don't think His Honor was feeling well that day; several times he pressed his hands against his temples or the stems of his glasses, as I do when I'm trying to cancel a headache.

Meanwhile Tabor finished consulting with Crain and came back to his post in front of us. He said in a low voice, "Okay, we're off and running." More loudly, to Coffey: "Did you at any time catch up with me?"

"Yes, sir." The grim-comic interlocution went on.

"Was I running fast?"

"As fast as you could in a small space like that, sir."

"But you caught me?"

"Yes, sir."

"So you ran faster?"

"I would say so, yes, sir."

"Have you ever run track?"

"Yes, sir."

"What did you run?"

"A quarter mile, sir."

"What was your time?"

"4:9 sir."

"That's pretty fast. I did 4:8.7 once. Did you at any time grab me or anything?"

Yes, Coffey had grabbed him, near a bed on which he told us a gun was lying, and said, "If you move, I'll blow your head off."

"You meant that, didn't you?"

"I certainly did, sir."

"You were kind of looking for an excuse to blow my head off, wasn't you?"

"If I was looking for an excuse, sir, I would have done it when I came in the door. . . ."

"Wouldn't it be fair to say that according to your testimony, my turning and running away from you with your guns directly pointed at me, was sufficient enough excuse for you to shoot?"

"No, sir. I was afraid of hitting the woman, sir."

"Very humanitarian of you."

"That's my job, sir."

There were more questions, about the policemen's lying to try to get the woman to open the door, and about the five- or ten-minute delay between the knocking and the entering.

The rich bitter drawl: "Detective Coffey, don't you think it sounds ab*surd* for you to swear under oath that I ran away from four guns pointed at me, knowing you were police officers, knowing the nature of police officers, knowing that you in*vade* our com*mun*ity and shoot us down like *dogs*—despite that, your testimony is that I turned and ran into the bedroom with *four guns* on me?"

"Mr. Tabor, I assume you are an intelligent man. You were hiding behind a pregnant woman knowing that we wouldn't use our guns while she was standing there. . . ."

"Isn't it a fact that you just made that asinine lie up in order to protect your lie?"

"No, sir."

At one point Tabor said, "Isn't it a fact that you harbor very ill will and adverse feelings towards myself and other members of the Black Panther Party?"

"Quite the contrary."

"You love us?"

The spectators rustled and snickered at this, and the Judge said, "I admonish the audience."

Richard Moore was not holding a gun when Sergeant Abraham and other cops came into his apartment and put handcuffs on him; but one detective told us he found a revolver on an outside window sill. On a table were some photocopies of papers with diagrams for making bombs, and the typewritten "book" called "Urban Warfare," by Kinshasa. Lefcourt asked Abraham if he knew whether Moore had ever read the book, and Abraham said he didn't. Moore did not have the machine gun that the police expected to find.

The Shakurs had no guns. A white detective told us that Lumumba opened the door; the detective shoved his shotgun into Lumumba's stomach and said, "Don't move." Afeni, like Tabor, questioned her own captor; she asked the detective, "Is that all you said?" The detective said, "Yes." Afeni said, "Mm-hm . . . Would it refresh your memory if I told you I'll never forget the look of hate on your face when you said, 'Don't move or I'll blow your fucking head off'?" The detective said, "I think you were in the bedroom at the time, and couldn't see me."

In their apartment the police said they found a large coil of orange fuse wire and some dismantled shotgun shells, with the bb pellets in an old milk carton. They took a five-foot spear and a bow with two arrows, but these weren't in evidence. Lefcourt asked the detective whether they found any weapons. "No," said the detective. "A bow and arrow?" said Lefcourt.

One of the cops who went to McKeiver's apartment said that they found the defendant in bed; he was not holding a weapon, but there was a pistol on a shelf above him, loaded. It was a Mauser, a handsome piece, as I found out when I examined it. The Irish detective who arrested McKeiver said he didn't know what the arrest was for, couldn't tell McKeiver what the charge was. The defense tried to get him to admit that the gun belonged to McKeiver's woman companion, but the Judge wouldn't allow the question.

Walter Johnson was not holding a weapon when he was arrested, but the policemen said they found some guns in the apartment.

Robert Collier had no weapons at his Lower East Side place. Besides his young daughter and his wife, who was weeping hysterically, there were two teen-age Puerto Rican fellows asleep on mattresses on the living-room floor, whom Collier evidently was sheltering and teaching English. Near them the police found three objects that the DA called "pipe bombs." We inspected them—six-inch lengths of plumbing pipe with screw-on caps; there was an "ashcan" firecracker in two of them, but otherwise they weren't loaded. There were also some pieces of copper tubing and, in the bathroom, a can of "smokeless pistol powder," we were told; we were given the can, empty, to examine. The cops had arrested the two Puerto Ricans; at the police station Collier said that the pipes were his, and the young men had nothing to do with any of it, so the cops released them. The arresting officer who told us this seemed to have some admiration for Collier.

In Dr. Curtis Powell's apartment the police, when they broke in, found some bottles of chemicals, which they took along, and books containing recipes for explosives.

At Ali Bey Hassan's Bronx apartment the police picked up a variety of "evidence"—newspapers, books, a decorated sword cane, along with a revolver and some ammunition. They even took posters from the wall, but the DA had not entered them as evidence.

Tabor asked Coffey about similar loot from his apartment. "Do you recall confiscating a poster of the Chairman of the Black Panther Party, Bobby Seale, and also on that poster the Minister of Defense of the Black Panther Party, Huey P. Newton?"

"Yes, sir."

"Uh, did you think that that picture of men taped to a wall was part of a conspiracy?"

The good detective swerved not. "Yes, sir."

"Why did you think the picture was part of the conspiracy?"

Weinstein objected to this question and the Judge sustained.

"Do you recall taking a poster with two black men at the 1968 Olympics standing upon the winners' platform with their arms outstretched in what is referred to as the black power salute?"

"Yes, sir."

Weinstein arose again. "Objection, Your Honor. So far as the People are concerned, these are all irrelevant."

"I think you're correct," said the Judge, "but I will allow it."

Tabor said, "You seized that picture also?"

"Yes sir."

"Did you know who those two black men were?"

"No, sir." Coffey, stalwart to the end, undoes himself.

"But you felt they were part of the conspiracy also, is that correct?"

"Yes, sir."

"You didn't take any fruit out of the refrigerator, did you?"

"No, sir."

"Fruit can't be engaged in conspiracy, that's why."

That wasn't a question, but Coffey said, "With a rock in it, I guess it could be."

To which Tabor said, "What?"

So Coffey repeated.

"Did you see any fruit in the refrigerator?"

"I didn't look in the refrigerator."

When Gerald Lefcourt was questioning Sergeant Abraham about his visit to Richard Moore's apartment, he said, "Now, at the time, the object of this mission was to get Mr. Moore, isn't that correct? . . . And that object was completed as soon as you opened the door, you had him, didn't you?"

Abraham said, "Well, partially it was completed . . . when we apprehended him, and we took the immediate material that was around him that would assist the District Attorney in presenting his case."

"The immediate material around him. Does that mean anywhere in that apartment, or does that mean where he was standing?"

"In the room, where he was standing."

"Did you take the rug?"

"No, we didn't need that."

Tabor to Coffey: "Would it be correct to say that you personally despised the Black Panther Party?"

"I despise the tactics, sir."

"Do you feel that it's your patriotic duty and obligation to assist in the elimination of the Black Panther Party and its members?"

"It's my duty to common decency, sir."

"Do you attribute predawn raids and the use of lies in the attempt to gain access into someone's home as being part of your common decency job?"

"Yes, sir."

Even at that early stage of the trial Tabor's message may have been getting to me: not so much the implication that Coffey wasn't giving the picture straight, as Tabor's dauntless facing up to his captor. I knew, however, that Tabor wasn't likely to take the witness stand and let himself be questioned; and nobody knew that a few months later he and Richard Moore would jump bail and disappear.

Tabor: "Would it be fair to say that you have a rather unique code of ethics?"

Young Weinstein stood up: "Objection, Your Honor."

The Court: "Sustained. . . ."

"After you seized me, threatened to blow my head off, told me I was under arrest, then what did you do?"

"I searched your apartment, sir."

"Did you find anything? . . ."

Coffey gestured toward the prosecutor's table. "Four guns sitting on that table, sir, a set of handcuffs, and some ammunition, sir." The guns were a P-38 automatic pistol, an M-14 automatic rifle, and two shotguns.

"Where was Miss Roslyn Bennett at this time?"

"She was in the bedroom, sir, wandering around."

"Were you informed during the briefing given to you by Inspector Knapp that there would be another occupant, another person, in that apartment?"

"Not to my knowledge, sir."

"But you did consider me dangerous; is that correct?"

"Extremely so, sir. . . ."

"And she was in the bedroom . . . roaming around?"

"Yes, sir."

"With guns there?"

"Yes, sir. . . . The woman was pregnant and she was scared half out of her wits. . . ."

"Would you say, officer, that a person who you perceive as being *scared* half out of their *wits* would be subject to pick up a gun and attempt to shoot anybody, especially *pigs invading* the apartment in which they are in?"

"Well, in this situation the possibility of that was remote, sir. . . ."

"Detective Coffey, isn't it a fact that I was seated in the kitchen in that apartment and that at no time did I ever go or was I ever taken into that bedroom?"

"You know that that is not a fact, sir. . . ."

Tabor held up one of the shotguns. "Do you recognize this gun, State's Exhibit 12—"

Wrong form. The Judge said, "People's Exhibit 12."

"State's exhibit," said Tabor.

"Mr. Tabor, you will refer to it by its proper name, which is People's Exhibit 12."

"Your Honor, uh, somehow I feel that we have different understanding of what the word *people* means, and who the *people* are."

"You have any understanding you wish, Mr. Tabor, but this Court has marked this as People's Exhibit 12 and it will be so referred to."

In one of the apartments there was a sawed-off shotgun. After a police gun expert described a sawed-off shotgun as "an easily concealed weapon," defense attorney Sanford Katz showed him and us that it was only three inches shorter than a regular shotgun, and the expert blandly admitted that it was no more easy to conceal.

Tabor's last question was, "Detective Coffey, isn't it a fact that you have been sitting up on that stand all this morning lying?"

Coffey said no, he had been telling the truth, and Tabor went back to his seat.

Detective Coffey had to be called back to the stand because one of the jurors sent the Judge a note that raised a problem. Coffey had said that a rifle supposedly found in Tabor's apartment was fully loaded; our inspection of the bullets that came with it, however, had revealed that they were blanks. So Coffey, on his return appearance said that he had used the term "fully loaded" because there was ammunition in the rifle—it didn't matter whether the shells were blanks or live.

People at the office, who read about it in the papers, asked me if I was the one who sent the note, and I said no. We learned later that it was Steve Chaberski, our political-science graduate student, who didn't want to admit it at first. As he also pointed out to us later, those bullets were not blanks in the ordinary sense of shells without bullets that did have explosive powder; they were "empty blanks" that did not even contain powder.

Lee Roper, carrying a book of Chairman Mao quotations, and William King were found in Columbus, Ohio, in November 1969. Near the end of the trial I realized that we had never heard about the April 2 arrests of Joan Bird and Clark Squire, because the police didn't find any evidence on or near them.

Chairman Mao
and a Bible

How far we were from standard television or movie investigations I saw in the first week of the trial when one of the detective-witnesses, telling us about the arrest of Richard Moore, said he knocked on the apartment door and heard a gun being cocked inside. A defense lawyer stood up and objected—the detective was not to conclude from the sound he heard that it was a gun being cocked! This legal nicety removed me (us), if nothing else had, from the filmed story in which the camera, if its director wishes, can sneak behind that door and show us someone cocking the gun. *The French Connection* is fun to watch because we in the audience learn that high-priced dope is being sold by the bad guys; the detectives have only dim clues and strong hunches until near the end of the story. Conditioned by such movies, by detective novels—which usually end with an outright confession in some form, to spare the reader the anticlimax of a court trial—I found it enlightening and burdensome that we were called upon to work with spoken testimony and solid evidence that was supposed to be limited by the judicial system, stripped of conclusions so that we, in the end, could weigh them fairly.

I had a mild tremor of doubt about the DA's case when he introduced as evidence the decorated souvenir sword cane that the police had "seized" at Ali Bey Hassan's apartment along with the revolver and Panther literature. The DA entered these things on the third day of the trial, and gave them to the jury to examine. Just like the movies: Exhibit X; the Court officer hands the gun to Ingram Fox and he passes it on; we each give it a look, a feel, a thought. (The three hunters on the jury always gave rifles a longer study, cocked them noisily and clicked the triggers.) Likewise the pieces of literature. Likewise the sword cane. I pulled the sword out of its sheath and ran the edge carefully along my wrist. It was blunt; so was the tip of the blade. Couldn't have been used for tenderized shish-kebab. *Cripes, Mr. Phillips —this is a Black Panther revolutionary conspiratorial weapon?* That's what I didn't say, didn't even let my face show.

I felt a little put-upon also while we examined the pair of handcuffs that a policeman said he found when they arrested Michael Tabor. The cuffs didn't seem to be worth much time, so I gave them a glance and handed them on to Fred Hills. I looked at other exhibits that Steve Chaberski passed to me—guns or bullets—and after some minutes I noticed that the defendants were stirring, whispering, smiling; a Court officer walked past, toward alternate juror Joe Rainato, who sat at the left end of my row; the spectators were whispering too.

Another officer walked over. Then Fred told me that Joe had locked one of the handcuffs onto his wrist. None of the officers had a key that would undo the cuffs. I could lean forward and look over to where Joe sat in embarrassment, with the reporters only a few feet away on the other side of the railing. Silence and decorum in the halls of justice were ruffled. (The next day's *New York Times* had a headline: "Panther Juror Handcuffs Self.") It was late afternoon; the Judge dismissed us so a locksmith could liberate Joe.

One of the criminally mischievous pieces of literature that the police found in Ali Bey Hassan's apartment was a copy of the newspaper the *Black Panther*, and it gave us another unconventional afternoon. Hassan had had several other editions, as the police admitted; but only one made it into the list of evidence, People's Exhibit 8. It contained an article about making bombs and hand grenades, which covered a small portion of the twenty-page newspaper.

Phillips asked the Judge whether he could read the article on explosives, aloud, to us. He had already, a day or two before, read us the entire "book" called "Urban Warfare" by Kinshasa, much of it about self-defense —not the most slam-bang opening for a trial. We were also allowed to peruse those literatures ourselves, of course, but Mr. Phillips no doubt wanted to make sure they were taken down by the Court reporter, and heard by the newspaper and television reporters in the audience. Judge Murtagh gave Phillips permission to read the

Black Panther article, and we sat through it. Then the newspaper was given to the jury to examine.

I was not a court buff, or a student of law, but I knew that when you found printed matter in someone's home you didn't take it for granted that he had (a) read it or (b) read all of it. You also don't take for granted that, if he had read it, he agreed with it. So I decided to go through the newspaper from front to back. Not a grand defiant decision, except that in a courtroom containing some 150 people it might seem a waste of time just to sit back and read for awhile.

As it turned out, most of the other jurors were thinking along the same lines. I didn't notice whether Ingram Fox perused the paper for long. Bill Beiser, history teacher, briefly scanned every page. Steve Chaberski spent some time on pages that didn't carry the explosive recipes. When he handed the paper to me, I looked through the headlined article on page one, which accused policemen, Jewish store owners, and Mafia of exploiting blacks. Inside, I read a few lines of verse, the hate-full message of which, in part, was that pigs should be offed. I looked over the rules for members of the Black Panther Party, which prohibited the possession of "narcotics or weed" while they were doing party work and the firing of weapons "unnecessarily or accidentally" at anyone.

Although the DA had made it superfluous for us to go through the article on explosives again, I scanned it enough to see that it had not been underlined or marked in any way to indicate that Ali Bey Hassan had read it.

Meanwhile, the other people in the courtroom were

biding their time. I thought the DA seemed a little surprised, maybe also the Judge, maybe there was surprise
on the part of the defendants and their attorneys—on
seeing that we were determined to de-select, de-choose,
our evidence.

I spent twenty or thirty minutes reading, interrupted
by lunch hour. Then I passed it on to Fred Hills, and
he read awhile. Fred handed it to Nils Rassmussen, our
Danish-born television film editor. The afternoon passed
in silence, except for low-keyed conversations here and
there in the courtroom. Fred and I chatted about R. D.
Laing and other current events. Fred somehow had a
theory about army food on his mind. "You know," he
said, "eating is one of man's most important concerns. It
seems to me that anyone who would opt to eat army
food all his life is somehow deficient." I agreed. "Although," I said, "if you get to be a colonel or a general
you can probably go to high-class restaurants. Maybe if
the army served gourmet food, refined people like you
and me would join up?"

So we waited, and the hands of the clock over the
rear door moved slowly. It struck me as funny, in a
serious way.

Another document that I perused briefly was a
mimeographed "Catechism of a Revolutionist"; a notice
at the end told the reader that it had been written by
Michael Alexander Bakunin long before the 1917 Rus-
sian Revolution. It had been updated with drawings of
blacks wielding guns. I don't think the DA ever officially
revealed its author or its vintage.

That afternoon was when I first felt the strain of not being able to talk about the case. The Judge had told us not to read about the trial in the newspapers, not to listen to radio or TV comments on it, not to discuss it among ourselves. *That sword cane is no weapon,* I wanted to mutter to someone. *What is proved by Lee Roper's carrying* Quotations from Chairman Mao Tse-tung *when he was arrested?* Among my friends, among my coworkers at the office (we had no court sessions on Fridays, the Muslim day of worship), I couldn't complain or wonder out loud.

When the little red book of Chairman Mao was passed among us (fortunately Mr. Phillips didn't read it for the record), I again had to decide: how do you examine a book that is in evidence? Don't you have to read it? I spent half an hour or so stubbornly scanning pages to see what Mao had said about bombing subways. The man who had seized this item when he arrested Lee Roper had to continue sitting in the witness box. (He was not a cop but a quite ordinary-looking FBI man who had found Roper and King in Columbus, Ohio, some months after the other arrests.) While I studied Mao, he read the Bible that was kept there for swearing in. I didn't read all the Quotations. One that caught my eye (I've checked it out in my own copy of the book) was: "To destroy the enemy means to disarm him or 'deprive him of the power to resist,' and does not mean to destroy every member of his forces physically." Also: "Communists must listen attentively to the views of people outside the Party. . . . If what they say is right, we ought to welcome it, and we should learn from their strong points; if it is wrong, we should let them finish what they are saying and then patiently explain things to them."

Everyone waited quietly while I read, but when we got our delayed recess a few jurors saw fit to make wry comments, and Obie Tunstall, one of the alternates, complained that I had caused him to miss eating the last half of his lunch sandwich.

Well, Obie Tunstall. Thin shrewd chatty black man, who worked for the Post Office. A study of juror types could focus as well on him as on any of us. But of course he wasn't a type, and if we all had anything in common—besides being acceptable to the prosecution and the defense—it was whatever made us willing to take on this job. It's not difficult to get out of jury duty: many of the prospective jurors, on learning that they would be excused if they said they had strong prejudices about the case, did say so. Some constellation of interests and ideals and curiosities had brought this particular group together. Obie was, like most of us, playful—surely one sign of sanity. "If you get sleepy in the jury box, Kennebeck, you should wear shades, so nobody can see your eyes." He satirically complained one morning that the counterman where he had stopped for breakfast gave him a *grilled* English muffin. "I asked for toasted, and he put it down on the grill." Or—not so playful—"You know, they say we should figure on paying one week's income as rent for an apartment every month. Well, where can I and my family find a large enough apartment for what I make in one week? And if we do find it, we probably won't get it if the land-lord is white."

Brief Recess (1)

It was a change for all of us. A change of life. New friends and new experiences that, unfortunately, we couldn't talk about. Editor Fred Hills and I, during the breaks, could comment on book matters and a few mutual friends in the publishing world. Joe Rainato, the dour-looking electrical engineer who was a reader of Communist literature, went with me to lunch in Chinatown—just a couple of blocks from the courthouse. He and I commented on the imposing and important declarations carved into our enormous building: JUSTICE IS THE FIRM AND CONTINUOUS DESIRE TO RENDER EVERY MAN HIS DUE. ONLY THE JUST MAN ENJOYS PEACE OF MIND. WHERE LAW ENDS THERE TYRANNY BEGINS. EVERY PLACE IS SAFE TO HIM WHO LIVES IN JUSTICE. BE JUST AND FEAR NOT. A regular stone anthology. One day Joe and I noticed a plaque at the rear entrance to the building saying that this site had once served as a station in the Underground Railroad.

Nils Rasmussen one day, as he was about to take his jury seat, showed me an old wad of gum that was stuck underneath. An enduring symbol of the American heritage—petrified through what eras of crime and punishment?

Although I seldom made notes in the jury box, I scribbled things down during our breaks, and at home I sat at my typewriter trying to recollect the events while I listened to music. Once I wondered, What if we had music in the courtroom? Crazy. For the DA, probably Mantovani strings and Tijuana Brass. For the defense, smacking guitar and hard drums. The Judge? I would give him Handel. It took me a couple of days to decide what the jury should have: surely the Charles Ives quartets.

At the office, one of the pretty secretaries, joking (I think), muttered "Pig" at me as I passed by. I laughed and said "Pinko" to her. Once she said, "What makes you think you can pass judgment on them?" I said, "Well, we'll be passing judgment on the DA too."

Sometimes we "real" jurors kidded the alternates about not having a say in the case. Murray Schneider would make as if to shove me out as I gazed through the jury room window. He and the other three extras said they would go ahead with their own deliberation and verdict. Of course all four of them hoped that fate would slot them into the real game.

Jury duty seemed to have special value in this phase of United States history, when so many citizens had no say in the direction of that history. The killings of Kent State students went unprosecuted, along with countless killings of blacks by white authorities. The fighting in Vietnam could not be stopped. Even—yes—crime in

the streets: its profound causes seemed hopelessly out
of control. Our chance to get the jury view put us exactly in the center of at least one problem, with the re-
sponsibility of making a decision about it. Jury duty
was a citizen's rare small opportunity not to be helpless
in the functions of the system.

"Speak into My Necktie, Please"

Gene Roberts, undercover agent. The drama of his arrival in the courtroom was especially rich, but the manner wasn't; the DA asked a Court officer to summon him, and he quietly walked in. He would give the first major testimony. Phillips and the defense lawyers had finished with the arresting officers. The DA had spent most of the morning showing us a typewritten Panther study outline (found in a defendant's apartment) evidently based on ideas in *The Battle of Algiers*. "Irrational hostile reaction," it said, and "Emotional Response (involuntary brutality)." It didn't seem like an aggressive view of revolution. I was thinking: This outline is about moving against oppression *if* it comes down from people in power—it's about self-defense. If the DA could miss its point, some of my fellow jurors possibly could too. That was bothering me, and Gene Roberts's stories didn't ease my beleaguered brain.

Roberts was in his early thirties, a good-looking man with a mustache. He was black, of course, a member of the Bureau of Special Services—the undercover

branch of the New York Police Department, also called
BOSS. His assignment was to join the Panthers, listen,
and watch. We learned, indirectly, a little about the
process by which the DA had presented his case to a
grand jury—the two dozen or so men who had the
power of deciding whether the DA's case was strong
enough for an indictment. Phillips had evidently brought
Gene Roberts and other spies before those gentlemen,
who could ask questions but of course did not have
the benefit of rebuttal by the suspected criminals themselves. I was astonished to learn that Gene Roberts had
appeared before them late in the night of April 1,
1969. The grand jury found the DA's accusations plausible, the indictment was prepared, and immediately the
arrest machinery was set in motion. There was a second
grand jury, as we learned, in October 1969, which heard
more testimony and saw more evidence, and brought a
"superseding indictment" that increased the number of
charges.

The DA had Gene Roberts begin by telling us
about an incident on the night of December 31, 1968.
On the sidewalk outside Black Panther headquarters in
Harlem, 2026 Seventh Avenue, around 11:00, Ali Bey
Hassan told Roberts and other Panthers that they were
to pair up and cut wires of some police call boxes. Hassan
(Roberts at first said it was Michael Tabor, but his
recollection changed on another day) passed out slips
of paper listing the boxes that each pair was to deal
with. Roberts told us that he and a man named Leroy
got a list of four locations and proceeded to make their

rounds. Roberts said he didn't do any wire cutting, but stood as lookout while Leroy did the job. Some of the defendants and spectators laughed derisively at this.

I said to myself, The DA will show us the official police records noting that some call boxes went out of commission that night. But Roberts went on to other dire tales, leaving that story to nag us. He told us that Afeni Shakur, at one of her section meetings, said everyone should get a handgun, and should pay dues of $2.00 a week for heavy artillery. She had an uncle who owned a construction company in Virginia, where she could get dynamite. At other meetings, he said, the Panthers talked of bombing subways, and Michael Tabor told him to "recon" the IRT station downtown at Worth Street. William King directed the group to get aerosol containers and five-gallon cans of gasoline for Molotov cocktails or aerosol bombs.

We didn't, of course, hear these stories as consecutive narration. They had to be filtered through the legal sieve, nerve-racking but necessary.

Roberts: "King stated that he preferred rubber cement and gasoline because the combination was highly inflammable."

DA (holding the daily reports that Roberts had typed up): "Did he say anything about Curtis Powell?"

Defense attorney Bloom: "Objection, leading, Your Honor."

Judge: "Overruled."

Roberts: "He stated that Powell was going to Jersey to pick up some gunpowder or chemicals to make the gunpowder with. He then went off telling how to make aerosol bombs. . . . He said for a shrapnel effect you would use bits of metal, nails, glass, thumbtacks, or what have you." (Suave-looking William King, across the room—are you regretting the nails and thumbtacks?)

Roberts told of nighttime "recons" he made with King and Lee Roper along the tracks of the New Haven Railroad. As they walked along the unlighted tracks, King pointed out strategic places for bombs—a switch, an underpass that happened to be near the back wall of a police station, so that explosions there would do double duty. On another night, Roberts took young Alex Mc-Keiver on a "recon" walk that turned out to be abortive—there were too many people walking around the railroad yard they had been told to survey. (McKeiver, light-skinned, listens without expression. How about all this, McKeiver?)

One day Roberts went with Walter Johnson to Macy's to look for places to plant time bombs during shopping hours. In the basement of Korvettes they noticed fuel supplies that could be set afire—"motor oil, transmission oil, butane canisters, propane canisters." In the gun department of Abercrombie and Fitch they saw weapons and ammunition that they could capture. At another time they reconned Bloomingdale's and Alexander's—two blocks from my office. (Walter Johnson's eyes slide from Roberts to the Judge, to the jurors, and down to papers on his table. Is he nervous, afraid, or just keyed up?)

On another night in the Bronx Botanical Garden,

Roberts said, he and four other Panthers sneaked around looking for places to attack—although King told them that Lumumba had said "not to do anything till around Easter."

Bloom: "Objection, hearsay."

Judge (denying the motion): "These statements are not taken for the truth of the matter contained therein, but as statements made in the nature of acts and done in the course of an alleged conspiracy." I'm listening—learning something more about law. "They are taken as to the defendants who said the words. They are taken as to the other defendants subject to connection, that connection being the jury's finding, if they so find, that a conspiracy was engaged in by the defendants or any of them. . . ."

The men searched through some shrubbery that March night, and climbed over the fence to get to a greenhouse, where King, Roberts, and Lee Roper checked for alarms. They saw two guards, and moved on to a supply house. "King said, 'We could put dynamite around this and blow the thing away.' "

They spotted an administration building and headed for it, wading through the waist-high water of the Bronx River. "We were wearing dark clothing with boots; I had on Marine combat boots. The others had on boots similar." Roberts hid in some shrubbery with two young Panthers (who weren't at our trial), while King and Roper "went around and took a look at the building." Then: "We went back across the river and went north-ward to an area that comes to about Bedford Parkway, or Mosholu Parkway, that runs through there. Then we split up and went our various ways."

Later, at the Panther meetings, Roberts and his companions talked about those expeditions and gauged the varieties of havoc to be generated throughout the city. They might spark a massive uprising if they could keep the police from sealing off the streets. Once Ali Bey Hassan wanted a match (for a cigarette? for pot?) and "McKeiver stated—laughed and stated, 'This reminded me of the time we were walking past the precinct and he also asked for a match, and King said, "I have only one; that's for the stuff." And Ali Bey said, "Give me a light off the fuse." ' "

Bloom objected: "Totally irrelevant and totally unclear. . . ."

DA: "Was anything said about where the stuff was?"

Bloom: "Objection—leading."

Judge: "Objection sustained."

But witness Roberts ignored the ruling. "McKeiver stated King had it in a vest pocket."

DA: "And did he describe the stuff in any other way than stuff?"

Roberts: "To my recollection, it was just stuff."

King once displayed a map with some markings on it—not in evidence. Roberts: "On the map, King had encircled sites along the New Haven Railroad, and he stated that these were the sites on the railroad that were to be hit. . . . There was also a police precinct encircled, and King stated that the police precinct would be the first target hit around 9:00 P.M., after which the railroad sites would be hit and the next day the stores would be hit—all of this before Easter."

Finally Roberts told us about the tiny microphone that he wore at some of the meetings and even during guerrilla exercises in Central Park. The microphone, taped to his chest under his shirt or dashiki or whatever, had a thin wire leading to a transmitter concealed under his belt. It broadcast the proceedings to two detectives in a car nearby with a couple of tape recorders.

During our breaks, our alternate Murray Schneider liked to say, "Speak into my necktie, please," and we laughed, but even now I can get a sinking feeling in my stomach as I imagine somebody wearing one of those at a business conference, say, or any group discussion. It was quite a sensational adventure—first time I had ever heard of a living person being "wired for sound," as Gerald Lefcourt put it.

The detectives in the car made their tape recordings. One of the eavesdroppers was a black man who looked over at us benevolently, instead of at the DA, as he explained the technicalities of the tapes he and his colleague had made—probably many more than we heard about. Only two reels got into the courtroom, and there was a lot of verbal battling before the Judge allowed them to be entered as evidence. We weren't present for these struggles; we sat around in the jury room, or we were dismissed and I went uptown to the Viking office. As I understand it, the DA played the tapes over a speaker and through earphones for the Judge, who at first decided that they weren't intelligible. Then the DA improved the equipment somehow, and got a tireless young fellow to type out a transcript. The tapes became clear enough to satisfy His Honor; one morning when we were called into the courtroom we had to step over thin cables on the floor, and each of us found a pair of headsets on the back of the jury seat.

Before we used them, we had to hear the young transcriber tell how, at the DA's behest, he had laboriously figured out each word on the tapes in order to type them. He said he did it with the help of Gene Roberts himself, along with Phillips and Weinstein. From the defense table Richard Moore said, "Murtagh could help." Finally we put the headsets on and started listening, supposedly to two evenings, March 11 and 13, 1969.

Harsh clanks and low-fidelity simultaneous voices jammed our ears, mixed with an incessant hollow roar like the oceanic sound in seashells. It gave me a fierce headache. We heard angry comments about revolution, guns, pigs, Chairman Mao. . . . Occasionally a distinctive voice came through, especially Tabor's. Since we had rarely heard the voices of the other defendants in the courtroom, we didn't know their quality. We didn't hear Afeni on the tapes at all, or any other woman.

One speaker who came through loud and clear was Gene Roberts himself. The mike on his chest was so faithful to him that when coffee was served at a meeting we heard his *gulp-aaah* as he swallowed. We also heard a wholly different personality: an eager and jivey Roberts with a hip drawl that he didn't use in the court-

room. "Yeah, dig it—dig it—dig it! . . . Don't start
Baba on that, cause you're going to get a long dissertation of the whyfors and wherenots!" Once, when they
talked about going into public places looking as inconspicuous as possible, he spoke of wearing an Afro wig
and his "Negro outfit"—meaning classy suit and tie—
"carrying a dictionary." He zealously offered to collect
a bunch of empty bottles, I suppose for Molotov-cocktail practice—"I can get Coke bottles or ginger ale bottles
—what kind do you want?"

We heard somebody recommending gasoline bombs
and other devices. In one remarkable bit, Roberts and his
comrades were actually huffing through some bushes in
Central Park. We heard Roberts's breathing. The Panthers often did physical exercise (push-ups, deep knee
bends), but this exploit was more likely "simulated guerrilla warfare." The men apparently emerged on a hill,
at night, near the uptown West Side corner of the park;
William King, panting a little, said that the intersection
of streets was a convenient spot for them to block off
traffic and harass any pigs who might be coming into
Harlem, maybe to quell a rebellion. King said that the
rooftops of Harlem had many wires, to trigger alarms in
police stations, so Panthers would have to be careful to
step over them. They talked about "laying shit" to blow
up subway tracks.

But there was also on the tapes a lot of boring discussion in someone's apartment about Chairman Mao's
prescriptions for revolution, and a lot of clatter as guns
were cocked and demonstrated and handed around, along

with laughter and good-natured shouting. Someone said that Easter (it was to fall on April 6 that year) would be a fitting time for violent activities because it was the anniversary of Bobby Hutton's death (in a shoot-out with cops in California). Somebody asked, "How about New Year's?" and started singing "Auld Lang Syne." When Lumumba or someone spoke of trying out Molotov cocktails in the Bronx Botanical Garden, a voice said, "Oh, my flowers! Oh, my flowers!"

Since the noise of those tapes nearly cracked my head, it must have discomforted the other jurors too. But we were all supremely attentive. We read through the transcript as we listened, page by page, and usually one of us raised a hand to signal that we wanted a page "replayed." Were the others, like me, looking for some operative conspiratorial words to supersede what Richard Moore called "shucking and jiving"?

Although the Panthers didn't speak specifically of killing people, their talk was spiked with threats ("You know the old match trick?" You mean when you take a match—" "Yeah. We're going to start a fire there . . ." —at Abercrombie and *Finch*, as they called it). I was reminded that Afeni Shakur, in her opening statement to us many weeks before, had said it was absurd to imagine that they would want to blow up stores like Macy's, where poor people did their shopping in the week before Easter. King at one point on the tape, however, was describing the damage that a dumdum bullet could cause: "It would be un-fucking-believable!"

The transcript we were following—only as an "assist," as the Judge pointed out—was fairly close, not always accurate. Some words, I could tell, hadn't been understood properly by the DA's transcriber. I was sure I heard one Panther speak of the cops' "braggadocio," but it wasn't on the typed page; and when King (presumably) was explaining the workings of a pistol, I heard him say, "The only automatic," but the script had "The only one advantage."

We were the jury though, we would interpret words and intentions for ourselves. The jury has the power, I said to myself. The power and the freedom. I didn't discern any real plottings on those tapes, no real plans in Roberts's reports. It seemed to me just wild talk, some of it inspired by *The Battle of Algiers* and other sources. Wild talk, bad blacks tossing around threats and insults, "playing the dozens" with the forces they thought were oppressing them.

The tapes were finished; the defense began their cross-examination. We learned that Roberts had a richer background than the other spies—had infiltrated Malcolm X's coterie so deeply that he was at the Audubon Ballroom in Harlem when Malcolm was assassinated there on February 21, 1965. He was, in fact, one of Malcolm's bodyguards.

Gerald Lefcourt brought this up, and apparently Phillips had decided to let his witness tell the story. Lefcourt: "Okay. What happened?" It was a dramatic moment. Roberts said that after the gunmen fired as Malcolm was beginning his speech, he ran down the aisle and threw a chair at one of them as they ran out; the man fired back at Roberts—missed him but hit his jacket. Outside in front, Roberts saw people kicking and stomping someone, then went back in and up to the stage, "where I proceeded to give Malcolm mouth-to-mouth resuscitation."

Lefcourt asked why Roberts had not testified in the trial of the alleged murderers. The DA objected to that question, and the Judge observed that there are often good reasons for such omissions. For one thing, I thought, Roberts wouldn't have been able to continue his disguised investigations; or, as they say, he would have blown his cover.

Earlier in his life, Roberts had been a buddy of William King's; they had attended junior high school together in the Bronx. Roberts became a member of the Black Panther Party in June 1968, at the very inception of the New York branch.

Roberts was articulate and reserved on the stand; he didn't go into the almost stammering weary wordplay that we were to hear from our "dynamite" witness, Ralph White. After a question he would pause, sit back expressionless as if he had forgotten where he was, then lean forward and give his answer.

As Lefcourt went on with his questions, we got new light on his stories. After Afeni told her group to contribute the weekly dues of $2.00 for heavy artillery, did Roberts ever pay? He said he thought he had, twice —$4.00. Lefcourt asked whether Roberts ever saw tanks or cannons among the Panthers, and the Judge scolded him for being sarcastic. Roberts said that no one was ever told to attack subway stations. He was never given an assignment to bomb anything. He never knew Afeni to go to Virginia to get dynamite. He was the only one of the group to acquire aerosol cans for making bombs. No one ever got the five-gallon gasoline cans that King had asked for.

Carol Lefcourt reminded Roberts of the remark about getting a light off a fuse—couldn't Ali Bey Hassan have been joking? Roberts didn't know.

When Sanford Katz questioned him, Roberts agreed that King had said they could, not would, put explosive charges under railroad switches. About that map on which King had encircled target sites on the New Haven railroad—it was a Shell road map. Katz produced one of these, unmarked, and asked about it, luring Roberts into muddy recollections:

Katz: "And did he have the map out on the table unfolded?"

Roberts: ". . . I believe he was just holding it up."

"In the air?"

"Sort of, yes."

"And how far away were you from him when he did that?"

"Not very far."

"But close enough so you could count six circles?"

"Yes."

"And you could read the print that was on the map, is that right, the location?"

"I can't recall whether you could see the print or not. The Spuyten Duyvil circle I had—I could tell from looking at maps before, the upper Bronx. . . ."

"Did it say Spuyten Duyvil?"

"I can't recall. . . ."

"How do you know it was Spuyten Duyvil?"

"Because I think that's the only area with twin peaks that the line runs through. I think there are tall peaks on each side of it. . . ."

"That's shown on the map, on the road map?"

"I don't believe it was."

In my humility I thought I had missed something, had failed to catch the word or phrase that provided a link of logic. But Katz was just as puzzled.

"So what does twin peaks have to do with the road map?"

"Well," said Roberts in the full flurry of his foul-up, "I have been on a few boat rides around Manhattan, and on Spuyten Duyvil there are these twin peaks."

"But did you understand my question, Detective Roberts? I didn't ask you what was located on Spuyten Duyvil, I just asked you how you knew it was Spuyten Duyvil area on the map that was circled?"

"Well, from the way it looked, I just figured it to be Spuyten Duyvil."

"I see . . . Well, when he held the map up in the air, was he discussing the sites?"

"To the best of my recollection, yes."

"And what sites do you recall his discussing?"

"Melrose, for one. . . ."

"Now, the map that you saw, did it have railroad lines on it or any marking that indicated a railroad?"

"I can't recall. I do recall the circle, though. . . . I believe they were railroad lines. I couldn't see the symbols for tracks."

"But you knew that the circles were around railroad lines, is that your testimony, from looking at the map?"

"Basically. . . . I know there is a railroad line that runs through the area, I think."

"But there was no railroad line as such on the map, was there?"

"Not that I can recall."

A short while later, Katz in his sharp voice, asked about the plot against department stores. "What was the day you agreed to bomb?"

"I don't recall any exact day being given," Roberts said.

"Which store was to be bombed?"

"Well, it had been agreed at a previous meeting that Macy's was a prime target or Bloomingdale's was a prime target; also at one meeting it was stated that Abercrombie and Fitch was the jackpot, or something to that effect."

"Well, by April 1, 1969, which store was to be bombed, which exact ones or one?"

"To the best of my knowledge, none been described as the exact one."

"And what type of explosive device was to be used?"

"To the best of my knowledge, none had been mentioned."

"And what time of the day or evening was this supposed to happen?"

"To the best of my knowledge, no particular day or evening time was mentioned."

"And which member of the security was assigned to which store?"

"To the best of my recollection, none."

We had heard details about Gene Roberts's last friendly excursion with the Panthers—an automobile ride to Baltimore on the night of March 31, 1969, with Moore, Tabor, and King, to pick up some weapons. They got to Baltimore around 7:30 in the morning, Roberts told us, and managed to get an M-1 rifle from a Captain Hart, along with some clips and blank cartridges. We heard nothing more about Captain Hart, who was probably a Panther official.

For such paltry pickings Baltimore seemed a long way to go. The defense got Roberts to admit that during their long auto trip King, Tabor, Moore—those three dedicated revolutionaries—didn't say a word about the Easter Plot. Roberts said he and the others returned to New York City around 11:30 A.M., April 1, and spent the rest of the day driving around town trying to get financing for another car and distributing the BPP newspaper. Around midnight Roberts went down to 100 Centre Street to talk to the grand jury, a few hours before his comrades were brought to the building in handcuffs.

Mind Reading

As I got to know my fellow jurors, our bland-blue jury room seemed to become more homey. It had no decor, there were fluorescent tubes overhead behind grilles like ice-cube trays, but to me it was a nice place, I liked going there. In our large courtroom the psychic and legal skirmishes tangled with physical discomforts —from heat or draft or bad light, or from tensions imploding in my head—so that when a break came I marched with the others gratefully through the short corridor into "our" room, and generally walked over to the nearer window to swing it outward and push my head into the grimy New York air. Occasionally I got fresh sparkling oxygen.

I looked down at the little park across the street, where shrubs and trees were shedding leaves, unmolested by the fenced-out public. Birds and an occasional cat inhabited it. On benches around its edges sat tramps, secretaries, attorneys, and defendants or their relatives from all the trials and hearings and confabs of that busy part of town. In the distance, through a small canyon of downtown buildings, a segment of the Hudson River glistened, and sometimes a boat pushed toward the Atlantic.

I didn't try to probe the other jurors' opinions directly, about Gene Roberts, tape recordings, guns, or anything else. Remarks between me and Fred Hills or Steve Chaberski in the courtroom, or with the others during the breaks, were about legal procedures if they concerned the trial at all, and didn't betray any strong impressions. I got used to the odd experience of suppressing my reactions to witnesses and lawyers and Judge.

Anyhow, before dynamite time with undercover agent Ralph White it all remained pretty open-ended, and I thought we might soon enough be knocked into clashing points of view. Better for everyone concerned to keep his cards hidden.

Still we must have been registering clues; sometime in the middle of the trial Murray Schneider, former grand juror, benign and humorous, said he felt that President Nixon's excursion into Laos would be useful in shortening the Vietnam war; this might have made me suspect him of undue favoritism toward the Establishment. (I said once that I wondered how much longer we could keep on shortening the war.) Some of the more liberal jurors now and then might have struck me as overly sympathetic to the revolutionary view. I didn't want any of the others to tell me what they were thinking, and if Joe Rainato, mechanical engineer, or Murray Schneider, employment counselor, might be almost bursting with some jokes or observations at lunch for or against the State of New York's case, I primly said that too much talk might cause a mistrial. I was probably being uptight about it, but the others agreed and changed the subject. For all I knew, my sense of propriety may have kept them from talking only around me, they could have been charting out the whole trial when they went off on their own—but I found out later they hadn't. Since Joe and Murray were both alternates, the problem was academic unless sickness or some other difficulty removed one of the principal jurors.

That possibility disturbed me also; I didn't want to break a leg, catch a cold that might turn into a prolonged illness, or otherwise jeopardize my privilege, my inside look at this contest between—what forces? The nature of the antagonists was not clear to me yet. I had to find out; we all did. Nobody could discover it more clearly, with more personal comprehension, than the jury. In fact we were, in a sense, to define those forces ourselves—at least, we were to determine where they stood at one local moment in history.

We had a range of definitions to choose from: some might see good policemen rounding up criminals, others an oppressive government purging revolutionary patriots. But we all must have had a strong sense that in this drama, though it didn't have the wide national reverberations of the 1969–1970 Chicago conspiracy trial, or the concrete implications of the New Haven trial in which Bobby Seale and Ericka Huggins were accused of complicity in murder—we were part of a major conflict between . . .

Lunchtime might have offered the most promising opportunity for mind-reading clues, but it never yielded any secrets that mattered. I had lunch with Joe Rainato more often than with anyone else, because we both liked Chinese food enormously. During the voir dire, Joe had told us all that he read Marx and Engels, and even that he had already formed an opinion on the case; he would, however, be able to set that opinion aside in order to render a just verdict if circumstances made it necessary. The DA must have decided to risk Joe's presence.

Joe was a bachelor in his mid-forties, engaged to a young woman he had known for a couple of years. Over hot and sour soup and mou-sei pork he and I talked about the villainies of capitalism. Oppression. Exploitation. Undeserved profits. The crime of Vietnam. I told him I hated sloganeering, on any side, I disliked even the idea of people shouting "Free Angela" if they didn't understand why she should be freed. Joe argued that basic necessities such as food and shelter were more important than the understanding of slogans. I said that my idea of a successful revolution was one that made everyone truly free—especially free to think for oneself. So our conversations went. Two idealists. At other times we talked about books—he read prodigiously, gluttonously—and I told him about book projects I had worked on at Viking.

When other jurors joined us, or me, for a Chinese lunch, I thought it would be fun to guage their open-mindedness by the kind of food they would try. Ingram Fox usually didn't venture beyond fried rice or chow mein. Claudette Sullivan, our vivacious, stylish woman alternate (black), also ordered some relatively safe dish like pepper steak. So would the other alternates, Obie Tunstall (black) and Murray Schneider (the only Jewish juror). Jim Butters, husky high-school shop teacher (white) in his early thirties, who came to court wearing Levi's and patterned silk shirts, had somewhat wider tastes like mine—chicken with walnuts, shredded pork with bean curd, egg-and-seaweed soup. Hiram Irizarry, the one Puerto Rican among us, played it safe, though. We couldn't persuade him or the other lunch-conservatives that in a splendid restaurant like Chi Mer, with its long list of Mandarin dishes, it was gauche to stick with the tried-and-true staples. I wasn't bold enough for cold jellyfish skin, and my one taste of sea cucumbers didn't excite me. Nils Rasmussen, the television film editor, was so quiet, reserved, that we didn't learn he too was a lover of Chinese food until the final weeks. He delved into the more exotic combinations sometimes, like kidneys in hot sauce. Some had martinis and such; our tongues loosened up, but our verdicts-in-the-making stayed locked in.

I had lunch with Steve Chaberski once or twice; he was willing to try something new, even if he might discover he didn't like it. It took Fred Hills some weeks to discover how good the Chinatown restaurants could be.

All clues to character?

But no, my food games didn't offer much amusement or enlightenment. I knew that a preference for french fries instead of bean sprouts had nothing to do with weighing legal evidence, and I early gave up my mild alarm over noticing that most of the jurors read the conservative *Daily News*.

Our only other woman, Eleter Yanes (black), in her fifties, always went her own way at lunchtime. Her job was downtown, at the New York State Insurance Fund, and she probably had office friends to visit. Miss Yanes (*Yan*-ess) endeared herself to us, however, with things to nibble on in the jury room—Jordan almonds or "chocolate straws" or cookies from her favorite downtown bakery. She, like the rest of us, had been calm and forthright in the witness box during her voir dire; but as soon as she was sworn in—number eight—the Judge declared a recess, and when she got into the jury room for the first time she sat down breathlessly and laughed and said, "It's like being on stage!" Miss Yanes—Nina—remained quiet during most of our breaks, sitting in a chair drawn near one of the windows, reading *Vogue*, *Women's Wear Daily*, *Variety*.

Bill Beiser, the tall, big-boned white man with the wide easy smile, was jovially enigmatic probably to most of us. To me he was a pure unknown quantity. He usually stayed in the jury room at lunchtime, eating from a metal lunch pail decorated with Day-Glo price and slogan stickers that his daughters liked to put on. I didn't know that during the voir dire Bill said he thought he might have to forfeit an assistantship at New York University, along with some credits that he could earn as payment, if he got on this case—"It would mean a great deal of inconvenience." Still, he was willing to do it. I missed his statement that the history classes he taught at New Lincoln high school, uptown, didn't cover events later than 1945, and that he himself didn't take much interest in things that had happened since that date. And I missed a terse exchange between Bill and Mr. Phillips:

Bill: "My original home is Algona, Iowa."

DA: "I guess you get a lot of kidding about that?"

Bill: "Not lately."

Bill, forty-two years old, had been away from Algona a long time, but he said "Golly," and was likely to utter—tongue slightly in cheek—such Iowa-isms as "I'm plumb tuckered out." He read paperback books on American history, which he toted around in a plastic bag. Like book editor Fred Hills, who often had business problems to resolve, Beiser had a lot of work to do as both teacher and graduate student.

I occasionally walked to the subway with him after the court session, but our conversations were about such matters as wintry weather, or faulty ventilation in the courtroom, or his own schedule problems that could arise if the trial went into, say, April (a possibility I could scarcely entertain). Bill lived in Greenwich Village, not far from me, but had to go far uptown in the morning to teach his 9:00 A.M. high-school class, then come further downtown to the courthouse by 10:30, when the sessions began.

Joseph Gary, black Post Office clerk, seemed to like strong and pollutey cigars better than food. We— Claudette Sullivan especially—coughed ostentatiously in the jury room and complained. "Where there's smoke there's Gary," I revealed. He laughed, puffed, stayed near one of the windows with Murray Schneider, who shared his addiction. Gary (he was never Joe) often stayed in at noon. Sometimes he asked me to bring back shrimps or egg rolls, commenting that the quality and quantity of food I brought him was much better than the Chinese dishes he got in Harlem. The first shrimps I delivered gave him trouble because I didn't bring a fork.

Gary, divorced, was in his good-looking forties, wore his graying hair in a short brush cut, talked in an agreeable high voice. He spoke of past girl friends, and talked to me about the races at Aqueduct, where I'd been a couple of times. He expressed very few political opinions. Sometimes he argued with Obie Tunstall, fellow Post Office employee, about the operations of the great mail service, and they told us some hair-raising tales of clerical carelessness, with that incredible humorous skeptical but not indifferent concern for the fate of the world that seems to characterize the best New Yorkers—the best Americans, maybe. Gary used to recall black families he had seen in shacks along the levees of the Mississippi; the people got flooded out frequently, he remarked with puzzled sympathy, but they wouldn't move away.

I remembered when defense attorney Sanford Katz was questioning Gary in the voir dire:

"Mr. Gary, I believe you told us that you had a chance to read the Black Panther paper but you didn't?"

"Right."

"What do you mean by that, someone offered it to you or—"

"Well," Gary said, "I was taking some people to the theater, you know, a show, and two kids were on the street, and so they said, 'Mister, you want to buy a paper?' I said, 'No, thank you.' And then I looked and I said, 'Well, yes.' I came back, and the one that asked me, I didn't get it from him, I got it from the other. So he says, '*I* asked you first,' you know. So I bought two of them."

Everyone laughed, and Katz, not sarcastic this time, remarked, "The wisdom of Solomon."

Then Katz said, "Now, you never read those papers, did you?"

Gary had put both papers in his back pocket, but later found they were missing. "I had intentions of reading, you know, but I never did."

"Someone else wanted to read it more than you did?"

"Maybe so."

Fred Hills sometimes went for a hamburger with Jim Butters. Although I didn't have lunch with Fred more than three or four times, I got to know him pretty well because he sat at my left in the jury box, in seat number five. He was elevated to the group the same day

I was, along with Nils Rasmussen, juror number six. (Steve Chaberski, the Columbia graduate student, was chosen later to replace the man excused from seat number three because of illness.)

Fred, in his mid-thirties, had curly sandy hair, a mustache, and horn-rimmed glasses. He wore well-fitted jazzy suits, shirt and tie and all, mainly because he went to his office every weekday before court time. "I've been working my ass off!" As an editor of the McGraw-Hill Book Company, in charge of college textbooks on sociology and science, he had achieved large managerial responsibilities shortly before his call to jury duty, so he had two burdens in addition to those of a husband and the father of two children. He and Bill Beiser and Nils Rasmussen (who went on weekends to his job at ABC-TV) must have poured more bloody sweat into those seven months than all the rest of us. Fred, even in the jury room during our breaks, usually sat at the table with sheets of paper in front of him on which he outlined plans for books.

My own situation at the Viking office was, happily, different. Besides being an occasional editor, I was in charge of the copy-editing department, with a staff of six bright, competent people who absorbed most of my obligations. I kept in touch by phoning in and going to the office on Fridays as well as during other court recesses, or by taking work home—once it was the manuscript of *Confessions of a White Racist*, Larry L. King's reminder that we are far from free and equal in the land of liberty.

Fred struck me as one of those high-keyed people who are constant critics of life, more positive than negative: evaluating, weighing, appreciating—whether it was some long-haired young woman who had just ambled down to the reporters' table (Jim Butters, behind him, corroborating: "Outta sight, man!"), or a business-suit gentleman sitting out there who might be a plainclothesman or an aide in the spy syndicate. Fred and I had time for innocent commentary during various intervals in the proceedings, not only while everyone else was reading Panther evidence, but also during side-bar conferences when lawyers gathered with the Judge at the far side of his bench to argue points that the jury wasn't supposed to be involved in. During one of these, when a lawyer said in a raised voice, "May I be heard, Your Honor?" Fred had to mutter, "You certainly can." When the DA called back a witness whom we hadn't seen for several weeks, the witness was reminded that he was still under oath. I asked Fred, "How long does it take for an oath to wear off?" and he said, "Until the promotion comes."

Although Steve Chaberski sat on my right in the jury box, I didn't get to know him as well as Fred; he was less gabby than I. He was the youngest of the group, twenty-eight years old; had done his graduate work in political science at Columbia and now was working on his doctoral dissertation. He said at the voir dire that, since his wife had a job—at an agency that referred parents of retarded children to sources of aid and advice—he was able to take on the jury schedule without much trouble. He had moderately long hair, a beard, a mustache. He too was difficult for me to read. In January he told me he would like to wear a short-hair wig into the courtroom, just to shake everybody up. I said, "Would you really have the gumption?" "Sure," he said. One pair of moccasins that he wore was coming out at toes and heels, which drew wisecracks from the wisecrackers among us—Butters, Hills, Tunstall. Steve, who had taken courses on the Supreme Court and other legal matters, had a special curiosity about the legal technicalities that were seething in front of us. He was the sort of man who might seem to get impatient with Ingram Fox's preference for protocol. Steve, say, impulsively wants to leave the jury room to get coffee downstairs; we've been waiting around nearly an hour, and we don't know what's going on in the courtroom. Fox gives the impression that he thinks we ought to make a formal request to Judge Murtagh. Steve just opens the jury room door, looks out into the corridor for a guard, and says, "Can we go for coffee?" The guard says, "Yes," and it's that simple. Steve makes a list of who wants what and leaves with Claudette and me as well, to help, and also to get out of the smoky room and stretch our legs.

Early in January we had a different set of Court officers for a few days who were less easy with us than our regulars; also, some of the courtroom clashes had been rough, and many of us probably felt keyed up. When Steve and I came back upstairs one morning with some cardboard trays holding containers of coffee, the guard at the courtroom's side door said, lightly but without smiling, "I might not let you in." Steve said, not lightly, "I'll throw this at ya."

As I look back I see that Steve did a great deal in an unobtrusive way, during our deliberations at the end of the trial, to keep harmonies flowing. I've said since that he might well become a politician, and I think I would vote for him.

Claudette Sullivan was another who didn't seem overly awed by the officials of New York State, although she was employed by some of them as a finance officer. She was in her mid-thirties, separated from her husband; pretty and vivacious, a black woman who had made good in the white man's world. I gathered that she went to Albany frequently to report to the State government on her department's finances and problems. While Miss Yanes was quiet and affectionate, Claudette was lively and affectionate—a proper woman, though—no revolutionary tones or attitudes, no racy language. She was New York born, endowed with the New York combination of irony and understanding. And enthusiasm; when I asked her once whether it wasn't frustrating to be an alternate juror, with not much chance of taking part in the deliberations, she said that it was, but she wouldn't miss this experience for anything.

Ben Giles and Charles Bowser were also mysteries; I didn't know where they went for lunch. I had the impression that Bowser, like Miss Yanes, had connections downtown. He was a light-skinned black man in his late forties. During the voir dire, Michael Tabor interrogated

him—as he and Afeni Shakur tended to do especially
with black candidates. "Have you ever experienced
racial prejudice?" Bowser's answer was simple: "I was
born in Washington." To me he was a slightly formidable man, very businesslike; in the jury room he read the
New York *Daily News*, with a cigarette dangling skep-
tically from his mouth; also paperback books—*Intern,
The Godfather*. He was a supervisor in the city Welfare Department (which didn't function well, he said
in the voir dire, because there wasn't enough money),
and also owned some real estate—apartments—in Manhattan. He seemed to know a lot about city affairs. He
made comments occasionally about newsy moments in
Judge Murtagh's background, most of which I unfortunately paid little attention to.

Then there was Jim Butters, thirty-two, born on
Staten Island, once in the Marines as a jet mechanic,
once a surfer in California, now a high-school shop
teacher of black and Puerto Rican students. He struck
me as elusive, during the voir dire, in his answers to
defense questions about whether any of the students at
his school were Black Panthers. At one point he seemed
sure that some were, and a little later he said he wouldn't
know. As to what he thought of the Black Panther Party
in general: "They are a well-disciplined organization,
and they are really an organization that's really bound
tight together." I remembered an exchange between him
and William Crain, who asked, "Do you believe that anyone has the right to overthrow the government?"

"Which government?"

Laughter.

"The United States government."

"The United States government as it is now, no."

If Bill Beiser was an unknown quantity because he said so little, Butters was an X because he had so many opinions, which he expounded with enthusiasm at lunch: he would defend his New Jersey property with a gun if necessary, law and order were what he stood for; or, he would offer his land for the use of poor people, he would share his good possessions in the hope of alleviating the pains that keep the world from peace. . . . He—later on in the trial—hated it, felt that it was like a bad LSD trip; yet he stayed on, showed up faithfully like the rest of us. He brought a chess set into the jury room and played with Ingram or Steve. He told me he and his wife had Charles Bowser out to their country acres one weekend to go hunting.

He and Bowser apparently got to be good friends; they sat next to each other in the jury box, behind me. Once, while the lawyers were huddled at a side-bar conference with the Judge, Butters mentioned to Bowser that he was thinking of growing a beard, but wasn't sure because he knew that patches of it would be white. Bowser, not in a whisper, said, "You'll come out looking like a goddamned Dalmatian." We all laughed, just as the lawyers finished their conference, and Phillips, who may have thought we had been listening in across the room, smiled grimly as he sat at his table and said, "I'm glad *someone* thinks it's funny."

Hiram Irizarry, maintenance man in a city apartment project (the one where Miss Yanes lived, in fact), was agreeable from the start. A smiling quiet man in his late thirties, with thick black hair and a mustache. Not fat, but maybe a little heavier than he should have been. We became friends early in our jury careers. He told me that Mrs. Irizarry wasn't happy about his new role because it took him from his regular place of work, which happened to be near where they lived. She had three small sons to care for—one had been born only nine months before. During the first two or three weeks Hiram worried about whether his salary would be paid through the trial. (Jurors got $12 a day, plus 60 cents carfare—a pittance by New York standards.) Later he learned that his money would continue to come.

Midway in the trial, as some of us walked toward a subway stop at the end of the day, I asked Hiram whether he got headaches like mine during the sessions. "No," he said, "I just get angry." I didn't ask him to expand on that. I remembered, though, a baffling dialogue during Hiram's voir dire. In answer to a question from defense attorney Bloom, Hiram said that, since coming to New York from Puerto Rico thirteen years before, he had *not* come to feel that there was discrimination in this country against black people.

Bloom said, "And do you feel that there's discrimination in this country as against people who are born in Puerto Rico?"

"No," said Hiram in his noticeable accent, "I don't think so either."

When Bloom had finished his questioning, he and

the other defense people went into a prolonged huddle. Then Katz came over, and after some questions and answers that seemed to change Hiram's opinions, said, "You think then there is, in some institutions, discrimination against Puerto Ricans?"

"Yes, there are," said Hiram.

"Then is it fair, sir, to say that you did not fully understand the question that was put to you by Mr. Bloom? . . ."

"Yes, I did."

Katz finished, and there was more private defense discussion. Lefcourt then came over, and asked Hiram about his languages. Hiram said he spoke both Spanish and English. "We try to speak English most of the time."

"Is that to try to get the family acclimated—"

"Right."

Later, Michael Tabor did some questioning. "You know what white racism is? . . ."

"No, I don't," said Hiram.

"Do you think that black people in America are treated fairly?"

"Yes. . . ."

"Do you think that Puerto Ricans are treated fairly?"

"Yes."

Then Carol Lefcourt, obviously sharing in the bafflement, asked, "Could you just tell me . . . if you think there is any discrimination against black people and Puerto Ricans? . . ."

"Yes, I think they have."

"Have you understood the previous questions that Mr. Tabor just asked you?"

"Yes."

"Can I ask you why you answered the two questions differently?"

The DA objected to this, and the Judge sustained the objection.

Carol Lefcourt: "You do think there is discrimination in housing?"

Hiram: "Yes."

"And jobs?"

"Yes."

The defendants and their lawyers again whispered together. As I watched Hiram in the witness box I was certain that he was not an ignorant or stupid man, nor was he trying deliberately to confuse the lawyers, to get himself dismissed. I could understand the defendants' perplexity. Maybe Hiram himself was confused, nervous.

The small drama continued when Lefcourt asked the Judge to excuse Hiram because he might not be able to understand all the English spoken in the trial. Although Lefcourt asked to discuss this out of Hiram's presence, the Judge would not allow it, so Lefcourt made his plea—tactfully, respectfully—with Hiram looking on. The Judge said that he thought Hiram was fully qualified to be a juror. It took a little more discussion at the defense tables to reach a decision not to use a peremptory challenge against him.

It didn't occur to me to ask Hiram, or even speculate

much, about his perplexing remarks on discrimination, because he turned out to be bright, responsive, far from inarticulate. I didn't think he had been bothered much by Lefcourt's request, but I wasn't absolutely sure— and the anger that Hiram spoke of could have been aimed at either side of the courtroom.

I might have hazarded one or two guesses about Fred Hills's opinion near the end of the trial, based on a few consonances that I sensed when we talked about other things; but, since he never voiced it directly, there was always severe doubt; for all I knew, he could have been putting me on, and he could have felt the same way about me. When matters as important as revolu- tionary conspiracy are at stake, when your opinion can get somebody sentenced to prison for a lifetime, amateur psychology doesn't help much.

There was a self-enforcing quality in the Judge's frequent warning: "The jury is admonished not to dis- cuss the case among yourselves or with anyone else. Throughout the trial you are to continue to maintain an open mind as to the guilt or innocence of the accused. If anyone should approach you to discuss the case, please avoid conversation. If he persists, report the matter to the Court." I didn't want to be caught saying or indicating some opinion that might get me bounced off the jury. In the courtroom we were hearing, day after day, stories of spies whose job was to report illegal-sounding re- marks. Many of us made cracks about the possibility of a microphone hidden in the jury room; there were odd-looking wires tacked to the baseboards and running into the Judge's chamber, which nobody really suspected. Murray Schneider liked to repeat his "Speak into my necktie" joke, but the funny aspect wasn't far from the spooky aspect. I thought it was likely that my phone at home was tapped. I'm sure that most of us were more careful to watch our tongues than the average jury is. I did not venture into Bloomingdale's, Alexander's, Macy's, or Korvettes after the Judge forbade us to visit scenes of alleged plots on our own.

Our deadpans got a lot of practice on the way to the courtroom. Waiting on a Greenwich Village subway platform in the morning for a downtown train, I occasionally saw Robert Bloom, who lived in my neighborhood. We would smile and make it a point to keep our distance. Claudette rode in the same subway car a couple of times with Richard Moore. She told us he stood near her once and said, "Aren't you afraid of me?" "No," she said. Otherwise, she and he kept their distance too. Once, at the courthouse, when an elevator door started to close in my face, Moore pressed the button to open it, so I stepped in and thanked him. He said, "Right on."

Up on the thirteenth floor there was usually a line of young, hippie-looking people outside the courtroom door, behind the sawhorse barricades; each spectator had to be searched before being admitted inside. They waited, patiently; we looked at them with half-smiles of recognition as the guard unlocked our privileged door leading to the jury room. But we had to be undemonstrative.

At a friend's Christmas party a distinguished old man who heard I was involved with the Panthers said, "I wouldn't give them any sympathy. They murder their own members." Instead of telling him that sympathy wasn't the point, that "they" is one of the most dangerous words in the language, I wished him a happy holiday. After all, *I* hadn't been so enlightened on the matter of American justice before the State of New York found me acceptable.

Week after week, day after day, the same defendants in their places, except that Tabor and Moore jumped bail ($100,000 and $50,000) in early February, and we would see no more of them; same scenario. There were hours of tedium. Some of us would almost nod off now and then, but since every point of testimony and evidence got a thorough going-over by both sides, none of us missed anything important. Late one afternoon, as Gene Roberts was murmuring about the plot to bomb New Haven railroad tracks, I improperly blurted out, "Your Honor, I'm sorry, I didn't hear the last statement." (I should have raised my hand first for permission to speak, but how are we supposed to know these things?) I think everyone was relieved at the interruption, and after Roberts repeated his remark the Judge adjourned us for the day.

Acceptable to the People?

Now it's the end of a trial day, we have been taken down in our special-privilege freight elevator operated by a gum-chewing friendly gray-haired woman. We go through the shabby-grandiose lobby, break up into groups to walk to subways, and will go to our separate lives until the next court session. As good a moment as any to think back to the voir dire, that initial movement in the justice machine that sorted and weighed and sized more than two hundred people to assemble this community of sixteen. It was the start of a major course in my Continuing Education: Socio-Psychology of Manhattan Tribes. The other candidates had emerged from the gamey or stylish, conformist or individualist multitudes of this peculiar enormous city, in tidy constellations of forty-two citizens, sent to the large courtroom, "Part XXXII," on the thirteenth floor, 100 Centre Street—to have their impartiality probed. Such a various variety: the movies couldn't get it right—not Hollywood, anyway, because these people had that firm substance and burnish that we call reality and hardly notice; it gives everyone a look of what you might consider ordinariness if you have seen too many "characters" acted out in movies.

A pleasant, sensible-looking, nicely dressed, thirty-ish woman (white), in answer to one of the usual questions, said she didn't think there was any racial discrimination in the South, except perhaps in Mississippi. Another white woman, also bright and alert, had worked with Judge Murtagh on a book he had written, had been his editor. She obviously admired him; in fact he may have felt embarrassed as she kept turning toward him before answering the questions, as if to see whether he was approving. His Honor was shrewd enough to disqualify her. The first woman had been peremptorily challenged by the defense—that is, dismissed without any stated reason.

Those peremptory challenges made the voir dire into a kind of perilous game. Either party might decide that a prospect had the wrong sympathies. The DA, hearing a white artist say that he had donated one of his paintings to some benefit for the Panthers, peremptorily challenged the man, who was dismissed without further discussion. The defense, after questioning a white man who wore an American flag lapel pin, challenged him. The Judge could not overrule those dismissals. The catch was that each side had only twenty peremptories. Catch-20? In this drama the defense used the most, the Black Panthers being a touchy issue even in the minds of some "liberals." As their peremptories mounted up to fifteen, sixteen, and they still hadn't achieved the full dozen jurors, it became more likely that they would have to accept some unsympathetic juror simply because he *said* he could set aside his convictions and follow the Judge's instructions. They must have felt that Kingman Brewster might yet be vindicated.

So as each new prospect stepped into the witness box, placed a hand on the Bible, and promised the clerk that he/she would "true answers make" to the attorneys' questions, those of us who had passed the exam watched and listened with quite a bit of interest mixed with suspense. "Mrs. So-and-so, is there any reason that you feel you could not serve fairly and impartially in this trial?" Then Mrs. S-&-S might say, "Yes, I don't believe that I could be fair." And usually the Judge would excuse the prospect.

Many others were on the stand for a great length of time, some of them more than an hour, as the several defense questioners dug around. A perplexing black man said that he didn't believe anyone under oath would lie. When an attorney asked him what he would think of two people who told contradictory stories under oath, he said that a person under oath might withhold something, or shade his comments, but could not deliberately lie to injure someone. When he was asked if he could judge the testimony of witnesses with the understanding that lying was possible, he said, "Do you mean at the end, when the jury decides?"

My impression was that he thought that some kind of divine power prevented people under oath from deliberately lying. (Well, why administer oaths otherwise, hey?) Judge Murtagh wasn't as baffled by this as I was, and as I think the defense people were. His Honor asked him if he would be able to follow instructions and deliberate fairly, and so forth. The man answered "Yes" because, I think, it was clear the Judge expected him to. The defense used a peremptory challenge on him.

To one black man, Afeni said, after several other questions, "Are you my brother?" He did not answer. Another man said he read the Panther newspaper. He was a young, vigorous fellow, who seemed to be chewing on something. Casual. What else did he read? "Well, *Post*, *News*, the Muslim paper, *Enquirer*, *Screw* —I read 'em all." The Judge: "I caution the audience to refrain from laughter."

But laughter was not thereby banished. Even the Judge succumbed to it now and then.

One seriocomic day, a Mrs. C. came on, middle-aged, once pretty, a forceful white clubwoman type who said she was a ghost writer of travel articles. She volunteered more comment than was necessary. When somebody asked for her views on violence, she said she thought it was childish. She gradually came to admit that she was extremely nervous about this case. She was sure she could be quite fair, but she considered the pressure to be terribly strong. What did she think of the Black Panthers? She said they reminded her of something exotic.

Michael Tabor stood up to question her. Strode over, spoke out in his deep bold accented voice. "Uh, you say that you find the words Black Panther exotic?"

"Yes. I'm an animal lover, and as soon as I hear Black Panther, I see a gorgeous animal."

"Do you find the defendants here gorgeous in any manner?"

"I haven't really looked them over."

"Well, Mrs. C., at this time would you please take the opportunity to look the defendants over?"

Phillips: "Objection."

Judge: "Sustained."

Tabor: "Do you find me exotic?"

Mrs. C.: "I think you're very attractive."

Tabor also asked her if she had ever heard of white racism, and she said, "I've heard of it, but I don't think it's half as important as it sounds."

She confessed she had never felt so nervous—"My heart's beating like a trip hammer"—yet *would* not say that she could not serve fairly. Lefcourt several times asked her about the "pressure" that she had mentioned. At least twice the defense tried to challenge her for cause; the Judge wouldn't allow it.

That was the time when McKinney came over and quietly said that he understood her nervousness, the feeling of pressure. But, he asked calmly and with sympathy, was there any comment that she would like to volunteer? At last she said that she would like to be excused. The Judge complied, and Mrs. C., cat-lover, walked out of our lives.

Fred said, "I think if she got on this jury she would make *me* nervous."

A black man who wore a suit and bright yellow shirt was an owner and manager of real estate: a landlord. He had some Panther tenants. Did he ever talk to them? Yes, about once a month. Laughter. After a lot of questions, both DA and defense found him acceptable. Everybody was set to see him sworn in, but he said, "I thought I made it clear that I can't serve here because of my business." With new rent-control laws, he had too many forms to fill out. The defense people conferred; Michael Tabor announced that if Mr. D. would have trouble running his building, he would arrange for the Panthers to take over the work. Amazing, I thought; the defendants would help a man who was sitting in judgment on some of their leaders. His Honor of course remarked that Tabor's offer wasn't legally proper, and Mr. D. said that maintenance wasn't the problem, it was the paper work, which he had to do himself.

Meanwhile, we slowly added occupants to the jury box. When we had eight jurors the defense had only eight peremptories left.

A white taxi driver underwent some lively questioning before he was dismissed. He seemed tough—heavyset, with a large scowling face. He may have had Italian or Spanish background. His straightforward comments must have said what a lot of prospects were thinking. "Let me state something. I'm uncomfortable in this position. . . . Having to probe my soul, I guess you would say, come up with decisions. . . . I am part of the system. I believe in the system, and now I am asked to participate in it, and like I say, it just leaves me uncomfortable, but I really don't know if I could do it. I would like to believe I could."

Mr. McKinney asked, "Are you suggesting, sir, that you would prefer not to be placed in that position, is that it?"

"No," the man said. "I'm saying—yes, that's the easy way out, isn't it?" But he didn't want to cop out of doing his duty. "I would if I had to."

I believed him when he said he could be fair-minded. The trial would make life difficult for him. He was the father of four children, and had to drive his cab to earn money. He would go from Court to the garage, and drive until midnight. It would mean just Court, work, sleep.

The defense asked him if he knew any blacks, and he said yes—as friends, as fellow cabdrivers, as members of a baseball team.

Tabor asked, "Would the fact that the defendants are totally opposed to the present system of government prejudice you in any way?"

"No, it wouldn't prejudice me any; I don't agree with it. I mean, I'll go along with the system; if you change it, I'll go along with that one." There was unsympathetic laughter.

"Do you believe that the American judicial system is a just one?"

"I've got to believe it."

When Tabor asked him whether he ever drove passengers into Harlem, he said, "I've never refused a fare—

and that's under oath." (The transcript has "that's on the road.")

But the defendants evidently didn't want to take a chance.

Another man failed to join our jury even though both sides found him acceptable. He was black, gentle. For forty years he had worked for the New Haven, now Penn Central, Railroad. His wife and daughter had both died. He had been on jury duty a couple of times before. There were lots of questions, and he seemed to answer them to everyone's satisfaction. But he said he couldn't take on such a long duty because he would not be paid during his absence from his job.

McKinney said, "You mean after forty years of service for a company, that you are in effect penalized for serving on a jury?"

"That's right," said the man, "never get paid."

"Was that your experience on the two previous occasions when you served on juries?"

"That's right. . . ."

"I think the union ought to do something about that, but be that as it may, would it cause you some economic hardship, sir?"

"Yes. . . ."

"Even during the days that you've been waiting on this panel, you have not been paid?"

"No. I took a week's vacation that's due to me, to attend."

Maybe the man was misinformed? Even so, the

union and the railroad should have told him. This bitter scene gave me a few long thoughts about our system, about the businesses that live on it, and off it, and in it. I felt especially glad then that my company took a more serious view of this duty.

I thought the defense misunderstood and mistreated another quiet black man who was employed by the Board of Education. He worked in the "central kitchen," in Queens, preparing sandwiches for lunch and sending them out to the schools. The trouble began when Gerald Lefcourt asked him whether he thought the presence of the defendants in court signified that they must have committed some crime. "What reason do you think they are here for?"

"Because somebody have done something. Whether it's any of them or who, somebody somewhere, I feel."

That seemed plain enough to me: somebody must have handled some guns, maybe some explosives—but for all I knew it could have been only cops. But the defense felt that the man didn't have a clear enough mind about it. When Bloom asked him about the defendants' presence, the man said, "By just looking at people I couldn't say that they done anything. I couldn't accuse them of something I didn't see them do with no reason, just because I see guns."

Bloom said, "Does the very presence of the weapons in itself influence you so that you could not evaluate the other testimony?"

"No, no more than I could believe that somebody

pushed something in my pocket and then I'm picked up for it. It could happen to me."

In my view the man was saying, "They could have been framed." But he seemed fairly indifferent to racial oppression. The defense peremptorily challenged him. The man didn't understand; he walked to a jury chair and sat down, until a court officer gently explained that he had been excused, and led him out.

Afeni questioned another black man who showed no strong concern over ghetto problems. She obviously didn't want this man sitting in judgment on her. I was dismayed when she said, "Have you ever heard the term 'house nigger'?" The DA objected to the question, and the Judge sustained. Afeni said, "Have you ever heard the term 'boot-licking lackey'?" Another objection was sustained, and Afeni ended her questioning.

Obie Tunstall's try-out as an alternate was short and snappy. Jeffrey Weinstein, who took over the questioning from Phillips for the alternate jurors, asked about the Black Panther newspaper. Obie said he had looked at it occasionally.

"How did you happen to see the paper?"

Obie answered as if someone had questioned the total of two plus two: "I bought it."

"On the street?" Weinstein asked.

"They sell them on every corner."

Weinstein's questioning lasted only a few minutes. The defense put their heads together for a moment, and Bloom, to my astonishment, said, "The defense has no

questions, Your Honor." Both sides found Obie acceptable, and there was a happy stir as he was sworn in.
Riding down in the elevator at the end of the day,
we were laughing at Obie's speedy triumph, but he
said he hadn't meant to give the impression that he was
all-out pro-Panther—"I read other papers too."

On October 15 the attorneys had filled all but the
last seat, number sixteen. It was a Thursday, and no
doubt everyone felt that, since we weren't meeting on
Fridays, it would be neat and expeditious if we could
get our man or woman before the long weekend. But
the day dragged on, and fate did not seem to be ready
to maneuver one more soul into our justice machine.
At 4:30—the time when the court session usually ended
—Mr. Murray Schneider ascended to the place of inqui-
sition. A stocky, sensible, agreeable-looking man, almost
cherubic. First came the usual suspense when the DA
asked whether the prospect thought he could serve fairly
and impartially, and so forth. At least from the first
answer we could often find out whether the prospect
wanted to be on the jury. Schneider said he could, would.
He worked for the New York State Employment
Service. He had served on a grand jury about three years
before: that sounded promising for the prosecution, not
so hot for the defense. Nonetheless Weinstein asked
Schneider many questions. The Judge said, "Is this an
example of brevity?"—maybe a reference to some side-
bar discussion that they had had. Phillips whispered,
"Finish, finish." Schneider was obviously acceptable to
the People.

Then the defense asked questions: Katz, McKinney, Crain. It got to be after five, but they weren't going to be hurried. The Judge was prolonging the day no doubt in the hope that the preliminaries—which had begun on September 8—would soon come to an end. Was Schneider one of the prejudiced fat cats? The defense attorneys were concerned about his grand jury stint. One of them asked whether his group had dismissed any cases? Yes. Had there been policemen testifying in some of the cases that were not dismissed? Yes. Would he evaluate police testimony the same as any other person's? Yes. Slow, careful. Question after question, as the clock moved. Nearly 5:30. Finally, did Schneider believe that a policeman could lie under oath? "Yes," said Schneider, "it's only human." After they finished, they conferred.

At last, both sides said Murray Schneider was acceptable. There were rustling and murmuring as he was sworn in and walked around to the sixteenth chair. The voir dire was over.

"I Can't Take It,
I Want to Quit!"

Gene Roberts started his testimony on November 10, his cross-examination began on December 2, and he didn't leave the stand until December 23. During November, we had to wait in the jury room for long periods while the parties were arguing whether Roberts's tape recordings were to be played for us. One day, after we had sat around for more than an hour, reading and intermittently talking, a Court officer summoned us —"Will you step in, please?"—and we filed to our seats, only to be told by Judge Murtagh that more discussions had to take place out of our presence, so we would be dismissed for the day. It was a lucky break for Ben Giles, because he hadn't been feeling well. He was our most senior citizen, a widower, sixty years old, retired longshoreman, black; the most quiet inhabitant of the jury room, who frequently rested his head on the table during the breaks and dozed.

Next morning we had another long wait. Ben had arrived in good time, and we asked him how he was feeling: ordinary human politeness, but it buzzed with a kind of family concern. He said he felt much better. "Nobody knows how bad I felt yesterday," he said. "Nobody knows how I felt, except me and my maker." I was sitting next to him at the table; he was more chatty than I'd ever seen him. He told me some sickness had hit him the day before as he was riding down to the courthouse on the subway. He had informed one of the clerks that he wasn't feeling well, and the clerk told the Judge, who passed a message back that he would recess the court if Mr. Giles wished. Although we were dismissed anyhow, I was relieved to hear about the Judge's offer; it meant that if one of us had a cold for a day or two, we probably wouldn't be in danger of being dismissed from service.

Ben told me he had gone home the day before and slept through the afternoon; his daughter said she wouldn't let her children bother him. I was delighted to find him so talkative. He was planning to go on a hunting trip that evening—it was Thursday—with some friends for the weekend. He told me that he had been a longshoreman for twenty-five years; he was able to retire in 1967 with a moderately comfortable income, tax-free. In his earlier years he had worked for a printer downtown in the courthouse vicinity—the company prepared letterheads and such. I was interested in this because I knew a little about printing. He had done some hand-setting, had taught himself to work a Linotype machine but wasn't able to get a job on one because he was black.

After the trial, he elaborated on this—said a white printer told him outright that niggers couldn't get that kind of work.

There were stronger vibrations traversing our jury room than I could sense.

That was a bright and chilly November day, exhilarating; inside, our conversations were remarkably animated and prolonged, as if the weeks of sizing each other up had produced favorable estimations all around. Across the table from me, Steve Chaberski and Bill Beiser were talking about U.S. history, especially the causes of the Civil War, because of some book that Beiser had. Jim Butters and Fred Hills were commenting on a murder trial that was getting a lot of attention in the papers. Someone talked about FBI investigations of antiwar protesters, and about other rumors that government agents instigated subversive plots in order to trap young people. Obie asked me jokingly who among us was wearing the mike. I said it must be Gary, in his bulky sweater. Obie went over to the window where Gary was smoking his cigar, patted him, said, "No, he's not the one."

Giles asked me to spell my last name, and I saw that he was making a list of jurors, as was Fred Hills. I told Giles a couple of names he asked for, and he laughed. "I should write a book," he said.

Which is what a lot of people said to me, at various times. I always told them I wasn't considering it seriously until the verdict was in. The lengthy notes I made at home every evening, including recollections of my jury colleagues, were part of my need to figure out what sort of people they were.

Claudette had been one of the pioneer icebreakers. After our four-day Thanksgiving break we learned that she had flown to Paris with some friends to spend the short holiday there—her first trip abroad. She came back with some French cold germs.

In my notes I wrote:

In that slightly augmented spirit of camaraderie that I felt today, is there also a reinforcement of my sense of skepticism among the jurors? A sense that quite a few of them share my doubts, so far, about the evidence? But I can't even pin down who among them seemed newly doubtful. Miss Yanes? Ben Giles? Mr. Bowser? (I have already, I think, sensed it in Steve and Fred and Joe.) Oh, also maybe Bill Beiser? And Jim Butters?

But I kept changing my assessments of nearly everybody.

What was I to make of our little conference in mid-December about the holiday schedule? Judge Murtagh, in the courtroom, had kindly asked the jury to let him know whether we agreed with his plan to hold sessions on only the first three days of Christmas and New Year's weeks. He recessed us then, to talk it over. The surprising thing was that Steve said, "We ought to think about the defendants." And Butters concurred: "Yeah, they have to be in jail on the days we don't have a session." So nobody disagreed when Steve suggested that we express our willingness to come in Monday through Thursday. As it ended up, the Judge stuck to the three-day week, however.

And yet: A few days later as I was walking down one of the main corridors with Ben Giles we noticed a black man being escorted in the opposite direction by two guards, with his hands cuffed in back. We stared. I said, "It's a shock to see someone in handcuffs, isn't it?" Giles said, "Well, if they're handcuffed, there must be a reason." "Not always, not always," I said, "it could be you or me." Giles laughed. "Yeah, it could be Mr. Rainato."

After the trial several people who had watched it told me that our loose-up was evident even to spectators. We might walk into the courtroom still laughing or smiling at some corny (or brilliant) remark, or finishing up a mouthful of Jordan almonds brought by Miss Yanes. Our clothes to some degree became more casual. Jim Butters eventually grew a beard. Joe Rainato let his hair grow a little longer than he ever had before, and also forsook neckties—even on some office days, he said. Since Butters and Chaberski and Gary seldom wore suits and ties, I took to wearing open-throat sport shirts (with suit jacket, though); they helped me to feel less tense and wrapped up. On days when we were dismissed from court unexpectedly, I went to the office thus dashingly attired.

Ingram Fox kept to his dark suits, with neat shirts and ties. So did Murray Schneider. Thin-man Obie Tunstall bounced around in conservative suits. Hiram Irizarry wore turtleneck shirts often, as did Nils Rasmussen, who, despite his remarkably formal bearing, had some fine knit outfits of mod cut. Fred Hills stayed with his elegant, colorful suits. Bill Beiser wore suit and tie on class days, and told us he deliberately dressed to set himself off from his students. *That* bothered me a little, since I favored educators who felt that a classroom should be free and equal. I wondered whether I had been wrong in listing Bill among the jury skeptics. He and I never happened to get into a discussion of classroom liberties.

Claudette Sullivan and Miss Yanes always wore good, handsome clothes—no slouch-look for either one. For quite a while I was under the impression that Claudette never wore the same outfit twice (I had the same impression of Afeni Shakur). She ran a gamut, excluding extremely maxi or mini skirts. It took her some weeks to work up the gumption to wear a pants suit, but wear it she did—so well that she needn't have worried about being found in contempt of anything.

Miss Yanes, in her fifties, had a more conservative look. She or anyone might be the cheerful brunt of trivial wisecracks about arriving late in the morning. Once when Claudette and Gary both came in at the same time, about fifteen minutes after everyone else, Charles Bowser or Obie Tunstall or Jim Butters made the obvious ho-ho comment, and Claudette pretended to be nonplussed. Gary sometimes would knock on our door before entering—a sound we associated with the Court officer's summons. Gary would enter and say, "Ha, ha, ha."

Murray Schneider suddenly puts down his paper and gets up, saying, "All right, once around the table," and Obie says, "Three laps," and Miss Yanes adds, "Your morning constitutional!" In the courtroom, Steve comments on an exceptionally good-looking female spectator and I say we might name her Miss Trial of 1971. I attributed the special quality of our looseness to the fact that we had had so much time to get to know each other, and had been through so many witnesses, so much "evidence," so many courtroom wrangles.

Wrangles were almost routine. The defense lawyers had a remarkable variety of styles, and in their zeal and anger, I daresay, sometimes went beyond the bounds of proper procedure. Phillips and Jeffrey Weinstein occasionally went astray, but for the most part they knew the rules well and seemed eager to stick to them. The Judge occasionally came down hard on Phillips, but he gave the defense lawyers a bad time with almost predictable frequency.

I got uptight-angry not so much at the quarreling as at some of the nonsense that it seemed to me the State of New York was asking us to swallow. My outrage, oozing from my head to my stomach, would spread tension into my feet, which I usually braced against the oak-paneled partition in front of us; I'm surprised that it didn't crash to the floor. There did come a moment when defense lawyers and the DA and the Judge were arguing so discordantly that Steve or someone cried out "Stop!"

Just after Christmas, Gene Roberts having been defused in my opinion by the defense cross-examination, the DA tried to expand our minds by instructing us in the relationship between bombs and subway switching "towers"—banks of switches that tell the trains where to go. One of the defendants, William King, had worked at a subway toll booth not far from the courthouse. Gene Roberts had told us about "reconning" that station with a view to planting explosives there. So, as my journal relates:

December 28. Back again after the festive days. Fred said: "Afeni did well at Christmas—look at that coat."

The DA produced a pleasant short round civilian, Isidore M. Berger, who gave his name in a low voice and murmuringly spelled it for the court reporter. Katz stood and said to the Judge, "Your Honor, we couldn't hear the name." The Judge said, "Isidore Berger." Fred said to me, "Never heard of him." At which I nearly broke up, but fortunately heaven has sent me a sore throat in which I can to some degree drown my laughter. It came in handy during the day.

The DA produced three large photos of the switching "tower"?—at the subway station that Roberts said he reconned. Mr. Berger is a specialist in such matters, who supervised the construction of this switch room in 1959. The photos were about two feet wide and a foot and a half high.

Berger explained how the switches work, holding the photos toward us, one at a time. Weinstein asked, "If any damage was done to the switches, what would hap-

*pen?" Objection from the defense. But Mr. Berger was
allowed to explain that if the board were burned or
blown up, the switches would not be able to trigger the
lights and switches on the track; the trains would stop;
there would be a great tie-up. ("Typical," I said to
Fred.) The main switching apparatus up at Grand Central
Station wouldn't be able to control the trains at this
station.*

It was elaborate!

Then came the cross-examination.

*After a couple of preliminary questions, Bloom said,
"In the spring of 1970, had any of these areas been damaged
by fire or explosion?"*

Berger: "No."

*Bloom: "You would have known about it if that
had happened—is that correct?"*

Berger: "Yes."

Bloom: "Thank you."

Witness excused.

I had to cough.

That same day Mr. Phillips brought us a bomb expert,
Detective Albert Gleason, a middle-aged white
man with a benign, tired face. The DA showed him and
us some aerosol cans and other so-called bomb materials
that police had found in the room where a Panther
named Eddie Joseph (Jamal) lived when they arrested
him. Joseph was not present at the trial because he was
too young. The cops' loot, besides the aerosol cans, included
an alarm clock with some wires attached, as if
for a time bomb. When it was being passed around the

jury, Charles Bowser made the alarm ring softly, twice. *Tinnnnng.*

The DA also brought out some evidence we had seen back in October—three so-called pipe bombs (containing two firecrackers but no gunpowder) found in Robert Collier's apartment, along with a red-labeled can that did contain some gunpowder. Also that Black Panther newspaper with the article on bombs. Also a book on explosives that had been found with one of the defendants. So Mr. Phillips succeeded in getting the mournful-looking Detective Gleason to scare us with scientific figures on what sort of explosions could be accomplished by certain amounts of gunpowder, gasoline, dynamite, and the like. (Dynamite, yes, even though secret agent Ralph White still hadn't told his story about it.) Sulphur. Blasting caps, electric and nonelectric. Firecrackers as fuses. Pipes, tubes, aerosol cans waiting to be loaded. When the DA lifted an ungainly white cloth bag containing those cans, Lumumba Shakur muttered, "Santa Claus!"

They were all ingredients which could be prepared and ignited to cause an "almost instantaneous change of matter into pressure," as Detective Gleason put it, "with the force equal to that of a hand grenade." If it exploded in a department store, the DA asked, would it kill people? Yes, in a crowded area the fragments would injure and kill people.

Aerosol cans taken from Eddie Joseph—there must have been ten or fifteen of them—went through our hands. The cops had found no explosives in them; most of them still contained liquids. Steve gave each one half a glimpse and handed it to me impatiently: "Pass 'em on, pass 'em on." I imagined that he shared my impression of silliness. I studied them, however. Glade Mist. Right Guard. Easy-Off. Some kind of lavender sachet scent. Many others. After we were through, the Court officer collected them and put them back into the Santa Claus bag, and the DA finished up. When William Crain later came over to cross-examine the detective who had seized them, he lifted the bag, clanked it noisily, and made a careful show of dumping the cans onto the DA's table. I said to Steve, "It looks like a supermarket." Apparently Eddie Joseph had been rooming with a Mrs. Baltimore; for all we knew, the cans could have been hers.

I wrote in my journal:

The DA is trying to plant possibilities in our heads. He is, in effect, telling us: "Just think of lousing up the subway switching center—think of the traffic tie-ups. Imagine it! You are all imaginative people, that's why we chose you for this jury. You're not run-of-the-mill, you've got imagination. Use it. We did!"

For some reason we missed a court session on the twenty-ninth, and Gleason with his bombing expertise continued on December 30. That last court day of 1970 we celebrated with more tales of fuses, powder, dynamite. The DA kept asking how much damage such-and-such a hypothetical blast could cause. The defense lawyers variously bobbed up to object to these scare hypotheses; the Judge kept overruling most of their objections, barking them down. At some point of tension His

Honor declared a brief recess. As usual, we got up and filed inexpressively past the Judge, past the defense tables, through two doors into our sunny room, and proceeded with our usual business of not talking about it. Except for handsome old Ben Giles. Suddenly he was standing by one of the windows saying, "Bulldozing! He's bulldozing them!" Referring to the Judge and the defense people. "I can't take it, I want to quit!"

Ingram Fox went to him, spoke some words of calm and comfort. Someone tried to give him a drink of Scotch. It had been brought in—the first and only time —I suppose to celebrate the last court day of the year; somebody had earlier suggested that it should be put out of sight and it was. But Ben doesn't drink. We settled down to reading, and after a few minutes Ben came to the table, where I happened to be, and sat down between me and Joe Rainato. Fuming, furious, he was muttering, "Not fair, he's riding right over them, I don't care if they take me off the jury—it doesn't mean that much to me." Rainato said quietly, "Stay on, you can be more effective that way." Giles was silent. Then, "Yeah, I . . . guess you're right," he said. I touched his arm and said, daringly, "Don't go—we need you."

That evening I wrote about the outburst in my journal: "Giles, who seemed conservative, has exploded. Has Giles been radicalized?"

A fun-filled December 30! It was the same day that Phillips said, "I would like the record to show that the defendant Afeni Shakur is singing." After lunch, Joe and

I happened to get on the elevator with Counselor Sanford Katz just as a woman elevator starter was doing a
quick clean-up; she kicked a wad of Kleenex out of the
car and picked up a long cigarette butt, muttering about
the sloppiness of people. She shoved a small candy carton out the door with her foot. Joe said, "That might
be contraband." "Yeah," she said, "it might be a bomb."
Katz said, "Let's not have any more of *those*." We tim-
idly laughed, but he didn't seem to be in a jovial mood.
Near the end of the day, as Gleason was still going on
about the big blam that five sticks of dynamite would
make, defendant Robert Collier spoke up—out of order,
of course—"Why not talk about a bomb that can kill
four children in a church? Talk about something real."

At this the Judge made an admonishment, and also
said it would be an appropriate time to break for the
day. He said we would reconvene on the morning of
January 4. "The Court extends to everyone best wishes
for a happy New Year." This brought jeers and laughs
and hisses from the spectators, and got a young white
woman in trouble for raising her fist in a power salute.
"Bring that lady forward," said the Judge. We missed
most of that incident, but after the trial we learned that
the Judge had fined her a couple of hundred dollars.

I made no such demonstration, but I was stewing
when I got down to the main lobby. I tried to phone the
office, to see if I was needed, since one or two copy-
editors had caught cold. The first phone I tried didn't
work; I didn't get my dime back. I went to another
phone and saw a sticker saying "Out of order." I went

across the lobby to another booth and put my dime in the slot. *After* I dialed, I got only a dial tone. I slammed the receiver against the wall, then put another dime in. No luck. I banged the receiver against the box four times, so hard that it hurt my wrist. It made a loud noise. I wanted to break that phone. Since it was the beginning of a holiday, there was nobody in the lobby to stare in alarm or arrest me.

Mutt and Jeff

Part of my anger may have been uncertainty. I had trouble trying to sort out some of the facts and my impressions of them, especially at the beginning of January, while we still awaited the revelations of undercover agent Ralph White and the dynamite story. I had not registered a clear impression of him when he had appeared briefly in November to say that Lumumba Shakur told him all Panthers should see *The Battle of Algiers*. As we watched the screening in the courtroom, with intermissions while the projectionist changed reels, White had sat in silence. Then he left the scene temporarily.

The DA had his own strange way of organizing the prosecution's case. He had thought that *The Battle of Algiers* would show us how the Panthers thought and operated. I hadn't seen it before. It made me understand all too well what feelings can drive people who think they are being oppressed. The film may have been loaded in favor of the Arab rebels and against the French establishment, as some critics said, but since we were seeing it under the DA's auspices I didn't resent the suspicion that it might be propaganda for the underdogs.

The torture and duplicity on both sides in the film were terrible, but the French appeared as the real villains. True, the rebels blew up milk bars where innocent children were present; rebel women smilingly deceived the French guards and got past them carrying murderous bombs in their handbags. But I think most of the select audience shared the rebels' elation as we learned of the ultimate defeat of the French. I'm sure the film did more to help me see things from the defense point of view than the DA suspected.

Now, in January, instead of getting White into the courtroom to tell us first how he replaced real dynamite with the phony sticks and then saw Lumumba doling the sticks out to other Panthers, Mr. Phillips was jumping across his chronology to explain where the three aborted bombing attempts left traces of the fake material. He didn't seem to be concerned about first "laying a foundation" for this fluorescent stuff; the foundation was to come later. The Judge said many times that we would get certain testimony and evidence "subject to connection": we would decide whether it was relevant to a conspiracy if we decided that there was a conspiracy. I wondered which side of the looking glass I was on.

We were to consider three sites. At a Board of Education building in Queens on the crucial night of January 17, 1969, a genuine explosion blew out a small chunk of wall outside a window, shortly after 9:00 P.M. At about the same time, also in Queens, a tiny bang went off at a police station directly across the Harlem River from Manhattan; the explosion was probably no stronger than a dynamite cap or a serious firecracker. From the debris of those two explosions the police said they picked up samples which, according to the DA's chemical experts, contained the material of White's fake dynamite: clay, oatmeal, a few bb pellets, and the fluorescent powder. This was supposed to be proof that the Panthers had put "bombs" there. I wondered what they had to do with the Easter Plot.

Phillips brought an ultraviolet lamp into the courtroom, had it set up on the ledge in front of our railing, and let us look at the debris, and it did indeed reveal large spots that glowed green-yellow and orange.

The third site of discovery was the back yard of a police station in upper Manhattan, the Twenty-fourth Precinct. Nothing exploded there, but a policeman on January 19—two days after the other incidents—found a paper bag containing five sticks on a grating in the parking yard behind the station. This policeman noticed that the fuse had been partially burned, and pinched it to make sure it was out. Then, thinking that it was the authentic explosive, so he said, he picked the bag up, carried it into the station, and phoned the Bomb Squad. No wily sleuth he, careful to let the dynamite lie exactly as he had found it so that his superiors could figure out how it got onto the grating. We were expected to decide that it had been put there by a Panther on January 17; Michael Tabor, reading about the find in the paper, supposedly remarked to another Panther that it had been lying there for two days.

The five sticks in the bag turned out to be phony,

too, the DA told us. We looked at them under the lamp and they glowed. To make us doubly sure of the chemical facts, the DA passed around some of Detective Gleason's unused raw materials in little brown envelopes. Clay. Fluorescent powder—some of it got on our hands and clothes, and the smears lighted up when we stood near the ultraviolet lamp. Oatmeal—"There's your breakfast," I said to Fred, who had rushed to Court that morning without eating; and Joe told me that Claudette, next to him, wondered whether it was instant or regular.

Soon after that we heard another upsetting story, the Harlem River Drive "shoot-out." This happened across the river from the small police precinct explosion, and the DA wanted us to decide that some Panthers had been caught near their red Dodge Dart just before they could snipe at cops whom they expected to run from the burning station, 1,175 feet away.

The DA showed us photographs (black and white) of the scene; he didn't try to have the Judge transport us all to that section of Manhattan's upper East Side, though that might have helped us visualize the episode better. The Forty-fourth Precinct station does loom up clearly across the river, as I saw after the trial. Phillips did bring into the courtroom a Police Department surveyor and map maker who displayed a large, simplified chart of the area where the red car had been parked, including the river, which ran along the east side of the roadway, and the Forty-fourth Precinct on an exposed rise of land beyond it. On the other side of the road were a grassy area

and a wooded slope, and on this wooded area the survey-
or had drawn a circle to locate a prominent rock outcrop;
prominent, and convenient for someone who needed a
solid vantage point for firing a rifle.

Attorney Katz asked the man some questions when
the DA was through, such as, why had he chosen that
particular outcrop to encircle?

"That was the only rock in the area?" said Katz.

"No, no," said the map man readily. "There are
other rocks."

"But that was the only point in this entire area . . .
that had a line of sight to the Forty-fourth Precinct?"

"No."

"There were others?"

"There were others, yes."

"But in your judgment that was the best?"

"That is correct."

"And so Mr. Phillips said, 'Put it on.' Is that correct?"

"That is correct."

None of the alleged snipers were traced to that
rock. The whole story seemed to be starting out wrong.

Sometimes the dates blurred in my mind, because it
was mid-January when the DA brought us this adventure, and the adventure itself had happened around the
same time two years before. On the night of January 17,
two highway patrolmen, not spies, had inadvertently become involved with the Panthers when they pulled off
the Drive, around 9:00, to see what was wrong with a
red Dodge Dart parked on the grass—so they told us.
They found two black young men who had gotten out

and begun to shoot at them. The cops fired back, and the Panthers scrambled up a wooded slope and disappeared. The two Panthers were Sekou and Kuwasi—names that we were to hear often. Then the cops found Joan Bird crouched on the floor under the steering wheel. They dragged her out and took her to their precinct station, the Thirty-fourth, for questioning. One of the detectives who had been at the station told us that, after talking to Joan, he may have asked the two cops whether they had "worked her over." The cops of course said no, but I was appalled that the detective, after seeing her bruised face (of which we were shown photos) might have casually asked such a question.

Since the cops had found a rifle in the trunk of the red car, the DA was trying to prove that the two escaped Panthers had been getting ready to use it in their sniping plot.

Now the story is getting hairy, I thought. This is no case of threats or plans. Those patrolmen are talking about real guns and bullets. One of the cops—he was a black too, named McKenzie—even noticed that his leather summons pouch had been pierced by a bullet. He had been wearing it at his hip during the gun fight, with a notebook inside. The summons pouch was given to us to examine, empty. We saw that it had two holes, all right, as if a bullet had taken a lateral path into one "edge" and out another, lower down. The pleated leather was so worn that a pencil could have punched through, but they also seemed to be the size of bullet holes. *Bad, bad.* Then the notebook was introduced, and I was all set to examine a bullet-ripped pad of paper; instead, we found it miraculously intact. The DA passed the pouch to us again, this time with the notebook inside. This was the occasion of a question from Steve. He raised a hand, and the Judge acknowledged it. Steve held the exhibit up and said directly to McKenzie, "Is this how the notebook was seated in the pouch?" McKenzie said it was.

McKenzie had told the grand jury that the bullet had gone "right through" the papers in the pouch; that's on the record. McKenzie had been mistaken. *Cripes.* The venerable jurors, I suppose, didn't ask to see those papers. Even one of the DA's own chemical experts added to my doubts. Bloom, in cross-examining him, asked whether a bullet could go through the pouch without damaging the contents. "No," said the expert.

There was a point where I could half-see that frenzy on the cold, dry grass beside the Drive, as the two patrolmen described it, both of them "scrambling" for cover behind their own car to duck bullets fired by the two "male Negroes." Then, cops firing their own guns, and Sekou and Kuwasi running off in different directions, up into the dark, leafless shrubbery and away while Joan Bird cowered under the steering wheel. But that picture really wasn't there to be seen. As the defense lawyers probed and prodded, the patrolmen each tried to tell us specifically where they scrambled to, and to make us understand how the young Panthers, firing revolvers at a distance of two or three feet, missed their victims entirely.

Later when we heard from other policemen and

detectives who examined the scene, we tried to understand why none of the Panthers' bullets were found in
the earth around the "scramble." Nothing else was
found, except a chrome-handled revolver among some
leaves and twigs. Fingerprints? We had moments of enlightenment as one police expert told us, at some length,
that it was *very* difficult to get fingerprints off most
surfaces.

Another expert did his best to explain that the
Panthers could have shot cops across the river with the
rifle even though it had no telescopic sight, its clip had
only three or four bullets (the cops weren't sure of the
number), and the whole sniping plot was supposed to
happen at night.

There was a lot of expert testimony. Fred said, "We
ought to start chanting, 'We want Detective White.'" I
said we could carry banners saying "No More Ballistics."

I had begun to realize that the only hard evidence
of a shoot-out was police photographs of the red car,
with bullet holes in the door—made by the cops' guns.
And three slugs (we looked at the twisted black cater-
pillars), found somewhere in the red car—from the cops'
guns. If I'm ever accused of shooting at someone, I said
to myself, I hope the evidence against me is no more than
bullets from *his* gun.

After Joan Bird was taken from this adventure to
the Thirty-fourth Precinct station in uptown Manhattan,
a detective named Delmar "Scotty" Watson supposedly
came there and persuaded Miss Bird to "confess." His

testimony about what she said must have raised an echo in Fred Hills's mind, as I was to discover the next morning.

To me, Watson was one of those assured and formidable men whose ruddy smiling smoldering faces can genially scare the daylights out of people who are timid or trapped or confused—or guilty. He was a relaxed but tough, efficient, red-haired man, apparently known to be expert at easing confessions out of balky witnesses. Attorney Katz asked him why he had been summoned that night to a precinct station that wasn't in his usual territory. Because, said wily Watson, Joan Bird hadn't been cooperative.

"You mean she wasn't talking?" Katz said.

"I mean she wasn't being cooperative."

"What do you mean by cooperative?"

"She wasn't giving information."

Joan Bird (perhaps bruised and terrified) calmed down and talked, Watson told us, after he asked her how she was doing and brought her coffee and other refreshments. She called him Scotty and he called her Joan. She told him she had been driving a car for the two Panthers, who said they had to be "at a certain place by a certain time." She was being tested. According to Joan (according to Scotty), the Black Panther Party was out to create "mad chaos" in the city and to "break the back of the law." Watson said that she never signed any statement or recorded her remarks on tape. We had to rely entirely on his recollection of the "conversation."

Katz: "Wasn't it an interrogation?"

Watson: "I call it conversation."

Katz: "Are all your interrogations conversations and all your conversations interrogations?"

Another exchange went:

Katz: "Can you tell the jury, Detective Watson, the secret of your charm in getting Miss Bird to—"

The Judge: "Counselor, I have admonished you throughout this trial that you are to refrain from sarcasm."

At any rate, Fred Hills, after hearing the allegations of beating followed by Scotty's gentle approach to Joan, must have been reminded of an article in one of the McGraw-Hill books he was familiar with. Next day he brought it to the jury room, a collection of readings on psychology, with a piece on police interrogation that discussed the "Mutt and Jeff" technique. When a mean cop, Mutt, fails to force a confession out of a suspect by violence or the threat of it, he is shooed away by a nice cop, Jeff, who gives the suspect sympathy and comfort. According to the article, this sense of release often leads the captive to spill out a "confession" that may or may not be reliable.

Fred made no comment when he brought the book in and pointed the article out to me. We discussed it in general terms; Claudette Sullivan got into the conversation and read the piece. So did Joe Rainato, and some of the others. We took it for what it was worth—an article that conceivably any one of us might have come across on our own. Then went on as usual to talk about something else—maybe the Vietnam war, tax increases, welfare costs, city employee layoffs, police brutality, sports, or movies. Anything but the questions that were jumping around in our heads.

The day we started hearing about the "shoot-out" happened to be the day Steve appeared among us for the first time without his beard. He still had a mustache and medium-long hair and casual clothes, and he looked younger. At lunchtime he said he had gotten a kick out of watching the lawyers react to his change of image. Lefcourt had noticed it first, and grinned. Fred Hills, who didn't quite realize the change until Steve mentioned it, said, "Well, I sensed that there was *something* different. I thought you had grown a mustache."

The story of the Harlem River caper fizzled past us. As I put it liltingly in my journal: "The only shooting that I'm sure of was done by the cops."

But I wrote a jittery reminder that the dynamite story was an attraction still coming.

Dynamite?

Ralph White at last came bopping into the court-room. "Where you been, boy?" whispered Fred Hills. Afeni and Lumumba Shakur made kissing noises. Dapper Ralph; or Yedwa Sudan, as he was known to the brothers and sisters; or Ralph Wyatt, as he was known to one of his girl friends.

He had a Mephistophelean look. Goatee and mustache; short-cropped black kinky hair with a slight widow's peak. He wore tight trousers and sport jacket, his detective badge pinned to the breast pocket. His voice had a strong, crisp tone, but the Court reporter often asked him to repeat his crammed-together words. I suppose he was nervous, but he smiled with remarkably bright teeth, sometimes glancing at his former comrades as if he might stroll over and slap palms and say, "Right on." Like Gene Roberts, as we learned, he had been preparing for this appearance, with the help of the DA, for a year or so; the rehearsals had probably been his regular job during that time, at regular pay.

I have tried to imagine White's life among the revolutionaries from June 1968 to March 1969 (he severed connections with them a short time before the arrests).

I get a clearer picture of him than of the other spies because he was the one who "saw" the dynamite, drank and smoked pot with the Panthers, and had affairs with a couple of women who were on the scene.

He was selected from the police ranks to join the Bureau of Special Services and become an infiltrator in June 1968, just a few months after he signed up. I can almost hear the orders from on high: *Watch for a Black Panther organization around New York.* In those days, J. Edgar Hoover and other authorities took the Panther rhetoric very seriously and thought that the party was terribly dangerous; some policemen in several parts of the county became so afraid of it that they went after a few members. Ralph White went to a Panther meeting in Brooklyn in June; not long afterward he was helping to set up a Harlem branch, under orders from Lumumba Shakur. Many of the other defendants hadn't joined yet.

He was buzzing around as the party grew, apparently active and zealous. He went to dinner at the Shakurs' sometimes, and at the homes of other Panthers who would eventually be defendants. He went to the security meetings, political-education meetings, physical training, guerilla-warfare exercises. And every day he secretly phoned police headquarters, where someone wrote down his observations. (Gene Roberts had written most of his own daily reports.) When Lumumba and others staged a rent strike in July at a tenement in Harlem, White was there; he reported Lumumba's brutal threats, and repeated them to us from the witness stand. In November 1968 Lumumba visited California, and when he got back told White that he had brought some "dynamite." Soon afterward, White listened while a few of his Panther buddies talked about something that "went down" at a police precinct station. The place had been bombed, according to the newspapers. There was nothing to connect our defendants to that November explosion except Lumumba's mention of dynamite, along with some newspaper clippings about the event that White said he found in Lumumba's desk much later at a place where they both worked. Defense attorneys asked White whether Lumumba, on his return from the Coast, might have been talking about marijuana, and he said he didn't know. I wonder whether the DA or the grand jury knew that "dynamite" was a common term for "terrific" or "sensational."

The place where White and Lumumba and other Panthers worked was called the Elsmere Tenants Council, with offices, such as they were, in a little one-story building in the Bronx. White was director of the project; he had been hired by a black woman he knew named Shirley Jones, who was over-all supervisor of the program—connected with the Office of Economic Opportunity—for the Bronx. White in turn had hired some of the Panthers. Thus it came about that he had three stations in life: as a police agent, an active Black Panther, and a city employee—BOSS, BPP, and OEO! Lumumba, White's superior in the party, was his employee at Elsmere. So were William King and a young man named Thomas Berry (Mshina), whose name we were to hear often although he was not on trial.

Shirley Jones wasn't a Panther, but she and White became intimate friends; he told us he had an affair with her.

The job of the Elsmere Tenants Council was to listen to complaints from people in the neighborhood about their apartments. White went to look at the places sometimes; he told us that the conditions were terrible. He was a concerned citizen. Those tenants didn't know their homes were being inspected by a Black Panther who was also a policeman.

Lumumba, in Moslem fashion, had two wives, Afeni and Sayeeda. Sayeeda, not on trial, evidently developed a romantic attachment to White; he said she wrote him some kind of love letter once, which he destroyed. Afeni, meanwhile, would goad him by asking whether he was a cop. Even Lumumba's brother Zayd told White he suspected him because his teeth were so good (as White told us).

The shabby Elsmere offices, a major setting in our drama, must have been bustling and noisy. We never did get a clear picture of what the place looked like, because it had been torn down sometime in February 1969 —soon after the work of the Tenants Council there was discontinued at White's suggestion. Apparently the DA, at the time, did not consider the place important enough for his photographers to record. But we did learn that it was a double storefront with an old davenport and some chairs in the entrance room for people to wait on, some desks, a soda-pop machine, another room with an upright piano and a desk where White presided, and random spaces in back, including a storeroom where, among other unused objects, seven tabletops were leaned together against a wall. There was also a small room with the very important refrigerator.

White and Mshina had used the back-room tabletops for "target practice" briefly in December. And on January 9, when White got uptight about some of Afeni's are-you-a-pig remarks, he stalked angrily back to the storeroom and—so he told us—fired his .45 revolver several times into the tabletops, by way of proving that he was a certified revolutionary. Five days later, according to White's peculiar story, Lumumba and Mshina were laughing about White's exploit, and about something else. Lumumba spoke to him. The DA: "Could you tell us, Officer, what the conversation was between you and Lumumba Shakur?"

White: "Yes. He said that there was some dynamite hidden behind the refrigerator at the Elsmere Tenants Council, and that I shouldn't do my thing. . . ."

"Can you tell us what doing your thing was?"

"Shooting behind the wall, because it is the opposite wall behind the dynamite. . . ."

"So it is fair to say that the dynamite was on one side of the wall and the tabletops on the other?"

"Yes, it is."

It was a disturbing story, another eyewitness tale

that we had to deal with, and I went home that evening with qualms jostling inside my head. But that last remark of White's turned out to be wrong. Gerald Lefcourt, when his turn came, asked White more questions about the layout of the offices, and in the absence of photographs even brought forth a rough sketch that Lumumba (I guessed) had drawn.

He handed the sketch to White. "I ask you if that is a fair representation, roughly, of the layout of the Elsmere Tenants Council. . . . I would offer it in evidence and ask the witness to correct it."

White looked the paper over, borrowed Lefcourt's pen to make a few changes. When the sketch was given to us we saw that he had altered the location of a few pieces of furniture. We also saw that the wall separating refrigerator from tabletops was not as White had described it. Now, by his own admission, there was a small toilet room between them.

To me this startling revelation came as a partial relief: something was indeed wrong. The DA showed no signs of discomfort; while we took our time examining the diagram, I saw that he was doodling musical notes—triplets—on his yellow pad.

Later, near the end of the trial, the defense brought Shirley Jones to the witness stand; she—obviously without any urging from Lefcourt, since it was plain that she was in the courtroom most reluctantly—said that the tabletops had always stood in an entirely different part of the room.

We had to contend with this hole in White's story. We had to contend with the possibility that it was a lapse of memory after two years, or that we had a liar on the witness stand, or . . . what?

Pirandello should be with us to concoct one more play about this adventure, the comedy or tragedy of trying to learn the truth through people's accounts of it. We had several witnesses to supply parts of this episode, but White was the only one who claimed to have seen the dynamite in a briefcase behind the refrigerator—if there was a briefcase behind the refrigerator. It was January 14, 1969, when Lumumba told White about it—if Lumumba did tell him. Later that day, White went back to the place to see whether Lumumba was putting him on. (He told us he went back around 7:00 P.M., but the defense lawyers got him to admit that he had told the grand jury he stayed at the office and checked it out around 5:00 P.M., as soon as everyone else had left. We were supposed to take the 7:00 P.M. time as definitive.) He said he moved the refrigerator aside and drew out the attaché case, in which he found twenty-four sticks of dynamite. He was able to describe the wrapping labels around the sticks, and how one of the clasps on the attaché case was broken and how he marked the position of the case on the floor with some broken broom straws, so he could replace it exactly.

He closed the briefcase, put it back. He didn't tell us whether he had trouble getting the refrigerator repositioned exactly right.

Then he went home, or somewhere, and informed his superiors. In the next few hours they cooked up the phony dynamite plan and told him what to do.

The next day, January 15, during office hours, White managed to glance behind the refrigerator to make sure the attaché case was still there. (If it was there, Signor Pirandello.) At the normal end of the working day he left. Late that night—2:00 A.M. on the sixteenth, in fact—he went back to the office. . . .

The DA, through his questioning and the detective's answers, wants to make us see a picture, a story. White takes the dynamite-filled attaché case from behind the refrigerator (leaving the straws in position) and puts it in a shopping bag and *takes a taxi* to a bus stop in upper Manhattan, where two detectives are waiting for him in a car. Dynamite that has been standing around a long time, we are told, crystallizes and is especially sensitive. Did the detectives know how fresh that batch was? With the dynamite, they drive downtown, three brave men, not worrying about their lives or the lives of the New Yorkers whose apartments they are passing.

When they get to the Bomb Squad Chemical Division on East Twentieth Street, they park in front and the two detectives carry the bag—gingerly? carelessly? laughing? nervously?—inside. Up some stairs?

The DA wants us to see them doing this. In the lab, another detective, Albert Gleason—as he himself told us—opens the attaché case, takes out the twenty-four sticks, and unwraps them. He substitutes the phony dynamite that he has made of clay, bb pellets, oatmeal, and the powder that will glow in colors under an ultraviolet lamp. Ralph White, downstairs in the car, is sleeping.

White's two detective friends bring the repacked briefcase down to the car about 4:30 A.M. and wake him. (He told us he checked the sticks and their wrappings and said they looked "horrible"—loose and sloppy.) The detectives drop White a block from the Elsmere office but they are able to see him go in the front door. Inside, unwatched, White puts the attaché case behind the refrigerator, using the straws as guides. He pushes the refrigerator back into place. When he comes outside, the detectives drive him to his apartment.

The DA wants us to see White seeing Lumumba, during the next two days, parceling out the dynamite in packets of about five sticks each, bound together with tape. (White told us how he watched nervously as this was done.) We are to imagine Lumumba and Thomas Berry and William King each going somewhere with a packet. But where? Does Lumumba, say, drive over to the Forty-fourth Precinct station on the night of January 17, sneak behind the building, light a fuse, and leave the (doctored) bomb on a roof over an adjoining shed? Does Berry go to the Queens Board of Education building and stuff his packet into a crack next to a window frame and light the fuse? Does King go to the Twenty-fourth Precinct station on the upper West Side of Manhattan, light his fuse, and toss the bomb (in a brown paper bag) into the back yard of the station? Lumumba's bomb doesn't work—only the cap goes off, or maybe a firecracker he was using as a primer. Berry's, somehow, has one real stick of dynamite (maybe Gleason lost count and goofed when he did his replacement trick?), and it goes off with a loud noise and blows a small hole in the wall. King's fizzles entirely, and lies there in the bag until a cop happens to spot it two days later.

While Lumumba is lighting his fuse behind the Forty-fourth Precinct station, Joan Bird and her two friends are parked across the river, getting ready to perform their roles in the plot. The two fellows get out of the red Dodge Dart and are ready to scramble up the hill with their (one) rifle, waiting for Lumumba's explosion; when the cops come running out of the station, they will snipe.

The DA did not try to tell us who placed what sticks of "dynamite" where; he couldn't tell us anything so specific: I've taken creative liberties with the Lumumba-Berry-King story. Three suspects in search of a witness.

We had only White's word that he actually placed the attaché case back behind the refrigerator: neither of the two detectives went with him into the Elsmere office as a witness. If, indeed, White did any of that. The grand jury evidently believed him. We had White's word that he saw Lumumba pass a bundle of sticks of dynamite to Thomas Berry; he told the grand jury only that he *assumed* Lumumba was passing dynamite. We had the word of policemen that they *found* a few luminescent handfuls of dust after the two explosions, and that five phony sticks that we saw glowing under the ultraviolet lamp had been *found* behind the Twenty-fourth Precinct station. We waited for someone who could say that he or she saw Lumumba or Berry or King —or anyone else—place dynamite anywhere, or even heard them plan to place it.

White liked to give us details that seemed to enhance his story. When he first carried the dynamite out of Elsmere, at 2:00 A.M., he attached a combination lock outside the door and left it at number 26, so that when he returned he would know whether anyone had touched it. He told us about those straws. He told us that he saw Lumumba give Berry a dynamite cap one day, in the Elsmere office. Berry, White recalled, put the cap into a cellophane wrapper from a box of Marlboro cigarettes and then inserted it into the empty box. Lefcourt, to my puzzlement, made a big issue out of this detail. He even brought forth an empty Marlboro box, with cellophane wrapper, to get White to demonstrate. Later, I saw why—Lefcourt read a passage about the same incident as told to the grand jury: White remembered seeing Berry wrap the dynamite "in a piece of plastic Baggie, you know, the Baggies; and it was placed inside the empty Marlboro cigarette box and put in his pocket."

We learned that White, like Gene Roberts, had worn a concealed microphone during Panther discussions on several occasions; but it brought us no tape recordings: too much static, or not enough bad talk?

I felt that my imagination was being stretched in many directions. It occurred to me that any rebel worth

his salt might hesitate to stash dynamite behind a refrigerator whose door was no doubt being opened and banged
shut by people thirsty for capitalist Cokes and so forth.
But that was only an amateur speculation.

Of course the discrepancies didn't come out all
at once; I had days of suspension between White's bald
original story and the slow, careful, sometimes tiresome
undermining of it—not really by the defense, but by
White himself as the persistent lawyers asked him
questions.

Afeni had a long colloquy with her former brother-
in-revolution. She was noticeably pregnant by then, and
showing her weariness. "I'm tired," she said angrily to
the Judge once. "Aren't *you* tired?" She ambled over to
our side of the room, leaned against the rail, and asked
White to explain a comment he had made that some
Panthers were "militant" while others were more concerned with problems in the community. Their dialogue
took on the tone of a good old theoretical rap between
comrades. I suppose all of us were fascinated. It was as
if White imagined himself once again at the Shakurs'
apartment or at Panther headquarters, with his grin, his
person-to-person gestures, the slight transformation in his
speech rhythms from formal direct address in the witness box to the zappy casualness of street talk.

Why, Afeni wanted to know, did White consider
her one of the militant ones? "What did you base that
on—my involvement? What involvement? . . . Tell
the jury what you saw me doing that gave you that—"

"You would go into a thing about pigs," White said, "and offing pigs, and different—things about offing pigs, and this pig is this, and this pig is that. . . . But you also spoke about the community. But I thought your military motivations were more so than political."

Afeni tried to get him back to her question—one of the trial's main questions: "We were talking about my actions more than my words."

White said, "I can't remember everything you said or everything that you had done, or even all your actions. . . ."

Afeni: "You said there are things that you saw me doing." Military-type things, she meant. "I just want to hear one thing."

White—probably getting as tired as Afeni after weeks of cross-examination—tripped over his words more and more as he continued his evasive maneuvers. I marvel that the Court reporters kept up with him as well as they did. (Why doesn't the Court use tape recordings too?) I'm quoting from the transcript: "I remember when—excuse me—I remember a meeting at the —I remember once at the Panther office, you were real charged up about—you went into a thing about icing the pigs, along that military thing, and very emotional." Then he commented on his own memory—observations that the grand jury probably did not have the benefit of. "I can't remember everything. I am only saying what I had based my opinions on, what I had seen. Then what I had seen and what I had heard, and I have forgotten most of them."

Then came an exchange that I wish Ingram Fox would set to music:

"Did you ever see me with a gun?" Afeni asked.

"No. I don't recall ever seeing you with a gun; no."

"Did you ever see me kill anyone?"

"No, I don't ever recall seeing you kill anyone."

"Did you ever see me bomb any place?"

"No, I have not."

"Rob anybody?"

"No, I have not."

"Never did any of that, did I?"

"I don't know. I didn't see you."

"I see," said Afeni. "Did you ever see me at Lincoln Hospital working?"

"Yes, I have."

"Did you ever see me at the schools working?"

"Yes, I have." I think White was beginning to appreciate the rhythm and forget what it might be doing to the DA's case.

"Did you ever see me in the street working?"

"Yes, I have."

"You remember those things?"

"Yes, I do."

"Are those some of the things that led you to believe that I was military-minded?"

"No, it was not."

"You don't remember the other things?"

White gave one of his Wonderland replies: "At the time I remembered them then. I remember—you reminded me of the *good* things that I saw you doing. If you could remind me of the bad things that you did, then I could answer that."

There was laughter as Afeni said, "Yes, I guess so." *

Charles McKinney walked over for the final questioning of White. He made a dramatic picture in his elegant dark-gray suit; his luxurious shirt had gray and white stripes and a large collar; his wide tie was pearly gray and pearly white, with a small circular pin of gems. He began with all the proprieties—"Sir, can you tell us . . ." His voice was controlled, his gestures firm, if slightly flamboyant, his stance composed. He generally stood far to our left, leaning against the rail that divided the reporters and spectators from us (he had been having trouble with his back). As his sense of contradiction grew, a tone of the revival preacher erupted sometimes—he barked his words and almost intoned his repetitious phrases. The Judge two or three times told him to modify his voice—he was not to argue with the witness. The points he went over were almost worn out, we had heard them more than once, but he made them illuminate the inadequacies of White's testimony, his recollection; and through White's answers he reminded us that secret police had begun to spy on the Black Panther Party as it was being established around New York in June 1968

---

* The Court transcript doesn't have White's last line right, so I have corrected it. The stenographers (white men), with their little silent magic machines, were bound to have a tough time sorting out phrases. White's remark as recorded doesn't make sense: "If you could remind me of the things that you said that I could answer that."

—before any criminal activity could possibly have occurred. McKinney asked White about his reports; for the busy day of January 17 and for two days thereafter, there were none at all. Not until January 20, 1969, after the aborted bombings, did the supervisors write down White's report that he had "seen" Lumumba passing out dynamite.

Finally McKinney got White to participate in another kind of choral drama as he asked, name by name, whether the detective had ever heard the defendants *agree* to kill anyone. Afeni Shakur? "No," said White. Lumumba Shakur? "No." Diminuendo: Richard Moore? "No." And so on, McKinney's rich voice modulating obviously and deliberately to a whisper with the final name: Clark Squire? "No," said White. "I have no further questions," said McKinney. The spectators sighed, and even the DA grinned in appreciation of the . . . performance.

The DA had no "redirect" questions for his witness. When I told Steve I was surprised at this, he said he wasn't. We didn't discuss it any further.

That evening I wrote in my journal: "The plot thins."

Brief Recess (2)

A February question: When is the defense going to finish with Ralph White?

He took all of that month. He had come in on January 26 and departed from our sight on March 2. Our lunches that week might have celebrated the end of a phase. On the next day Joe, Nils, Claudette, Ingram, Obie, and I went to the "beef-stew place," as Claudette called it because of its Wednesday specialty. It was an ordinary bar across the park behind the courthouse, on the fringe of Chinatown. We might have been celebrating, if our attitudes toward White had been overt enough. As it was, that lunch came about just as randomly as any others, and was as casually genial. The bartender, and two or three other burly white men who sat drinking, greeted Obie and especially Claudette as if the two had been regular customers for years. The beef stew was said to be good, but neither Joe nor I ever got it because there was never any left on the days we went. The alternative ravioli was not as good as our favorite Mandarin dishes, but the camaraderie made up for that.

In the jury room, Fox would tell me with bouncing

enthusiasm about his opera or some Carnegie Hall recital he and his wife had gone to. Nina Yanes and I compared judgments on *Coco*, *Company*, and other shows. Fred Hills and I occasionally did a *New York Times* crossword puzzle, with help from Joe Rainato.

I met three attractive jury wives. Vidia Rasmussen, from India, edited a magazine called *India Abroad*. Fred Hills's wife Patricia, soon to become an associate curator at the Whitney Museum, was working on her doctorate, had two children to care for, and nonetheless visited the courtroom several times. Laraine Chaberski had lunch with some of us—Chinese fried dumplings at the Dumpling House. The lunches, around 1:00 P.M., got livelier and livelier; then, back to the jury room by 2:15, into our usual chairs—everyone tended to have his/her own place at the table or against the wall or near a window— to continue the kidding around or read or talk.

The spirit of playfulness bounced from Obie to Claudette to Gary to almost everyone. After a break in our jury room, the Court officer opens the door and says, "Would you step in, please." Claudette interrupts her conversation with Fox, shows mock annoyance, says, "I'm not ready yet." During another break, on a rare occasion when we have to summon an officer for some reason, we decide to use the wall buzzer. "I want to push it—let me do it!" insists Claudette, so whoever is standing near it steps out of the way. Even in the courtroom the tensions sometimes relaxed: while Sanford Katz was grilling a witness one day the DA sneezed, and when Katz said "God bless you" the DA thanked him.

Obie, during the incursion into Laos that wasn't supposed to involve any U.S. ground troops: "Say, I wonder—when those American helicopters take Vietnamese soldiers into Laos, do they touch the ground, or do they have to stay one foot above it?"

Fred, as we file out of the courtroom after a tiresome afternoon: "We should wear buttons that say 'Free the Panther jury.'"

Only during one of the final weeks did I have lunch with Bowser, at an Italian place that Butters and Rainato and Fox led us to. Charles Bowser turned into Charlie during that hour. We had white wine and red wine, and contributed later to the level of drowsiness in the courtroom.

Jim Butters, at lunch one day deep into March, told me he was getting damn sick of the trial. He was anxious to take his wife (beautiful Toni, whom I met after it was over), to some island where they would be unfindable for a couple of weeks. We were now hearing from Carlos Ashwood, the fourth undercover agent. The third, Lester Eggleston, a large, older man with a beard, took the stand for only a few minutes early in the month, quoting two minor statements by Robert Collier that didn't amount to anything.

March:

"How many more spies do we have?"

"One more after Ashwood?" The DA, during his opening statement, had dramatically pointed out five who were sitting in the courtroom, and each one stood up as Phillips gave his name. We had yet to hear from the one named Raymond Fulton.

"And then the defense will have to bring *their* witnesses."

"Will the defense have witnesses?"

"Do you think the defendants will take the stand?"

"Can one of them take the stand without the others having to?"

"Will the Judge dismiss the alternate jurors before deliberations, or will they get to hang around?"

It turned out that Ashwood was our last spy. We never did hear from Fulton.

"What Do You Call
a Plan?"

I had a strong emotional reaction to Carlos Ashwood—intensely negative—and it bolstered my hopes a
little to see that some of the others were put off by
him too. One morning, as Giles and I were walking
down the corridor with Claudette, she remarked that he
was the most uncooperative witness of them all. I thought
that Fred felt the same way. But Steve Chaberski seemed
to admire Ashwood's spiky manners. And so I began to
be bothered about now-beardless Steve.

Carlos Ashwood (also known as Carl Wood) was
thirty-one, almost chubby, with a trace of double chin.
He had a dark round face with a mustache. His speech
had echoes of a Spanish accent; he had been born in
Panama in 1940, came to the United States in 1947, had
served in the air force for four years, joined the New
York Police Department early in 1968, and by July of
that year was a BOSS agent posing as a Panther.

He began his direct testimony on March 3. This
time it was Phillips's assistant Jeffrey Weinstein who
asked the questions. Weinstein was a young man with

black wavy hair and delicate features; his fingers were long and slim. He dressed with proper elegance, and I thought he looked much more like a violinist than a prosecutor. His session with Ashwood ended on the next day, but the defense, probing, probing, kept Ashwood on the stand, with small interruptions, until March 30.

Ashwood seemed to me a strangely *private* man, not the noisily manic type that Ralph White may have been, but with an introverted confusion of soul, as I might put it if I were his spiritual adviser. During the trial, as we came and went, we had occasionally seen witnesses waiting around in their bare waiting room or in a corridor "backstage," and would exchange polite smiles with them. Ashwood I found it impossible to smile at; which may have been unfair. I only know that on the witness stand he disconcerted me with his long pauses before and during replies and with the fierce resentment he seemed to feel at defense questions. He may well have been embarrassed and angry because the attorneys asked why he hadn't been promoted to detective along with Ralph White and Gene Roberts; but I thought he behaved, much of the time, almost as if he took it for granted that he had been hired to get convictions rather than simply report his observations.

As I look back, however, I wonder whether he might have been baffled by his role in the trial. He had seen certain Panther comings and goings on January 17 (the night of the red Dodge Dart), which may have struck him as mischievous but more or less routine, and now the knowledge that his minor observations were meant to bolster the DA's grand charge of conspiracy may have shaken his soul profoundly.

Who knows? Probably not even Ashwood. *He* never heard anyone talking at length about dynamite or an Easter Revolution.

Ashwood had ridden in the red Dodge Dart a short time before it turned up in the Harlem River Drive shooting; the car was rented to defendant Clark Squire. Ashwood had been at the Shakurs' apartment in upper Manhattan on the evening of January 17. He and several others ate some chicken quickly, because they were on their way to a Black Arts Festival at the Harlem ballroom called Rockland Palace. The festival was sponsored by a rival organization, Ron Karenga's "US," but the Panthers had a table in the lobby where they were offering their literature. Carlos Ashwood was assigned to preside over the concession. Ashwood told us that Lumumba drove him and Clark Squire to Rockland Palace in the red car, and dropped them off, along with some Panther newspapers and posters. Then Lumumba drove away. That was around 8:45, not long before Joan and two other Panthers in the car encountered the patrolmen. Nobody ever tried to tell us where Lumumba went, or when he turned the car over to Joan and her friends.

Ashwood apparently hung around the ballroom lobby until midnight. Inside, various entertainments and speeches were going on; the Last Poets performed, but we didn't learn much else about the program. Around

10:00 P.M. Alex McKeiver came in and said to Ashwood, "The thing didn't go right. I don't know what happened."

At about 10:50, Mshina came in—one of the fellows who had supposedly gotten some of the fake dynamite from Lumumba as Ralph White watched; he was nervous, upset. Around 11:30, Lumumba and Afeni came in with Ali Bey Hassan and Sekou, who was presumably still shaken up from the "shoot-out," which Ashwood didn't know about. Sekou, although his companion Kuwasi had evidently fled elsewhere, didn't exactly seem to be in hiding. He was limping, however, Ashwood told us—further evidence of some mishap. Ali Bey, who seemed to have been running, also said that things hadn't gone right.

Ashwood didn't know what all that talk and traffic meant; he was unable to remember whether any of the Panthers that night specifically mentioned police stations, shooting, dynamite—keep the revolution a secret from the revolutionaries! Even his police superiors hadn't told him to be looking or listening for clues about the dynamite that Ralph White had discovered a couple of days earlier. Ashwood may have been mightily bewildered by some of the defense questions.

The DA would like us to see a picture of the conspiring Panthers straggling into the Rockland Palace lobby, disappointed because their dynamite had fizzled in three places; Sekou scared and breathless from his encounter around the red Dodge Dart; Ali Bey Hassan baffled over some goof-up in his part of the plot. But we didn't get enough scenery or dialogue through Phillips to fill it out.

Ashwood seemed not to have heard about Joan Bird's arrest that night, and did not phone police headquarters immediately to report that his buddies must have been up to something serious. In fact, he said that after he left Rockland Palace around midnight, he met Joan's sister Rosemary; they stopped at a bar for a drink and then went to her apartment because—because Rosemary wanted him to help her clean a couple of guns. Which they did. Tunstall and Bowser laughed about that in the jury room, as the atmosphere continued to loosen up in some quarters.

Ashwood, like the other spies, told us that he had gone to meetings where he heard the Panthers rapping about bombs and guns and ammunition—also called TE, technical equipment. He repeated Gene Roberts's story that Afeni said she would go to Virginia to get dynamite. He backed up Roberts's story about cutting call-box wires on New Year's Eve. Ashwood, however, admitted cutting wires himself at one place. The man he was with also cut wires but was never arrested for it, as far as he knew—although he was able to give the man's name. Thus we learned that the only corroborated act of insurrection was done by a policeman with an accomplice. McKinney rhetorically asked Ashwood whether he was on trial, and Ashwood said, "That's a matter of opinion," which amused most of us, including the Judge.

There were several funny moments in Ashwood's

testimony, which I could have enjoyed if he hadn't been such a dismaying witness. On the evening of April 2, for example, after most of the defendants had been arrested, he was still hanging around Panther headquarters in Harlem. Lee Roper was there, too, uncaptured. When Roper learned that he was on the indictment, he asked Ashwood to lend him money for a taxi, and Ashwood offered to ride downtown with him. Roper said, "No, I don't want to get you involved in this." The secret agent lent the fugitive some money, and apparently didn't make an effort to give his fellow police any information to help nab him.

The date of April 2 meant nothing special to Ashwood. At one point he said that he saw Roper give Richard Moore a revolver on that day, forgetting that Moore was in jail by then. He had trouble with other dates, too, even January 17. He needed his voluminous "notes" to refresh his shaky recollection even more than the others had: these were reports which he, like White, had usually phoned in, to someone else who wrote them down and, possibly, adjusted them here and there for the sake of clarity or completeness or . . . law and order. (Throughout the trial, the spies' use of their reports, and defense lawyers' questions about the contents, set off many of the noisiest courtroom quarrels.) Maybe Ashwood just didn't have an "aptitude" for dates. Maybe he hadn't done massive rehearsing for the trial, as Roberts and White evidently had.

Katz asked Ashwood if he had attended a "section meeting" on a certain evening. Ashwood asked to look at his report, since he wasn't sure of the date. Katz, instead, read from Weinstein's direct examination, in which Ashwood had indeed told of a meeting on that day. So he had to agree that he had been to a meeting then, if the record showed that he said he did. Katz asked whether the Panthers had talked about arresting a pig at the meeting. Ashwood, with his blank stare: "At what meeting, Counselor?"

And Katz asked him whether he had received any special police advice for his spy job. Was he told to report somewhere every day for instructions? No, said canny Ashwood, he was not ordered to report every day. But when Katz asked him how often he got instructions, he said, "Every day." The catch, apparently, was that he received some instructions by telephone, so he wasn't "reporting" anywhere.

Ashwood kept up this verbal ducking-dodging. It seemed to come from him effortlessly. If he were a boxer he might win by driving his opponent crazy. Hour after hour of it almost made me blow my cover as an undemonstrative juror. I developed a habit of staring at him. At that round dark face, those insouciant but unrelaxed eyes, the peculiar laconic performance.

Sanford Katz, I thought, was extraordinarily patient with this spy. Sometimes, when Ashwood gave one of his nonanswers, Katz tensely raised his hands, like a pianist about to begin, then dropped them. I imagined the blast of anger that Katz may have allowed to subside without venting. Steve Chaberski, though, continued to admire Ashwood's unflapped endurance.

When Katz was asking about the Rockland Palace evening, Ashwood repeated one of his observations: "Sekou walked by the table. He was limping. . . ."

"Well," said Katz, "as he was walking by, did you notice any cuts or bruises on him?"

Ashwood, on a note of conversational triumph: "He was wearing long pants, sir. He was limping."

Katz: "Well, did he have a mask over his face?"

Ashwood didn't answer.

Katz: "Did you notice his face?"

On a higher note of triumph, Ashwood said, "Yes, I noticed his face. That's how come I knew it was Sekou."

Steve laughed at this, but I was appalled.

Katz wasn't the only attorney to move his hands in the air. Robert Bloom did too, and once the Judge asked him to stop it. So Bloom stuck his hands in his pockets and continued talking. The DA, though, fanned his hands around many times before and after that, without offending the Judge. Bloom's beaming face was an effective courtroom device; the Judge once said, "The record will reflect that Mr. Bloom is smirking." (I don't think Bloom ever smirks.) A little later, when Ashwood made a funny remark, Bloom said, "The record will reflect that the Judge is smiling." Fred Hills whispered to me, "No, that was a smirk." Since the Court reporter can't depict facial expressions in his transcripts, the Judge got the record clear by saying that he was not smiling—was, in fact, feeling very grim.

Ashwood, like his buddies, admitted that he never heard any defendants agree to bomb department stores, subway stations, railroads, police stations. ("Why don't we all go home?" said one of the defendants.) But when Afeni questioned him, he went back to dodging. She asked him whether he ever heard her plan to bomb the New Haven Railroad. He said, "Mrs. Shakur, that is a matter—what do you call a plan, you know?" Afeni said, "Ask the District Attorney. He has us on trial, not me, baby."

Pipe Bombs?

On the last day of March we had to sit around the jury room for a couple of hours, a relaxed bunch of captives. Butters played chess with Steve, while Ingram Fox looked on, offering pointers and friendly arguments. Obie and Bowser, joking about some of the spies' testimony, were getting a little out of bounds, I thought. There had been one case of a detective who told us he spent many weeks looking for Sekou after he ran from the "shoot-out" on January 17. Yet we had heard Ralph White describe some of Sekou's comings and goings during that period; he had been traceable up to April 2, when he escaped arrest. "Would it annoy you," one of the defense lawyers asked the detective, "to find out that the Bureau of Special Services knew where he was every minute, and that you wasted all your time?" This Obie found funny, along with Carlos Ashwood's statement that, after cleaning guns with Rosemary Bird on the night of January 17, he went to his cover apartment first, in case he was being followed, then went to his real apartment, where his wife was—apparently not thinking he could be followed *there*. Obie liked to imitate Ralph White's boppy style of walking, to the amusement of Joe Rainato and Ben Giles and Bill Beiser. Nils laughed a little. Others, like Miss Yanes and Murray Schneider, preferred to maintain silence. Steve remained enigmatic, to me at least.

Another weird story from Ashwood and White was that some of the Panthers had "gone underground" after the January 17 thing—supposedly because they were afraid of being arrested for their crimes. I had no difficulty believing that they may have been talking in those terms, but the DA's seriousness about it came to seem ludicrous. As the defense lawyers probed, we learned that these hiders-out were seen at Panther meetings, at the apartments of friends, in the streets; one of them, Robert Collier, even appeared on a WBAI radio interview. Ashwood at one point quoted someone as saying that Ralph White was "semiunderground." (We also gathered that Lumumba Shakur and Clark Squire had gone voluntarily to the Thirty-fourth Precinct station late on the night of January 17, to inquire about Joan Bird. Apparently they were arrested and soon released.) I tried to neutralize my smile as Obie and one or two of the others rehearsed these absurdities.

Hiram Irizarry and I, standing at one of the windows, looked at construction men working on a building beyond the small park, and tried to estimate whether they were as far away as the Forty-fourth Precinct was from the Harlem River Drive. I said, "Could you hit one of those men with a gun from here?" Hiram said, "Maybe if it was a machine gun I could."

We could all feel the end coming, though we would

have been distressed to know that there were six more weeks ahead.

There was at least one other story that some of the jurors might have been brooding over. The DA had interrupted Ashwood's appearance to bring us a witness named Richard Brown—a young fellow with light brown skin who wore a white turtleneck shirt; with him came a young, pretty white woman, his lawyer, who sat near the witness box. He was there to tell us that late one night in February or March 1969 some Black Panthers had picked him up at his Brooklyn apartment, along with a friend of his named Roland Hayes. He and Hayes were driven into Manhattan, to an apartment on the lower East Side, where Robert Collier and some others, including Curtis Powell, brandished a pistol and berated Roland Hayes for giving them bad dynamite. Hayes said no, he had gotten the dynamite in Vermont, it was good stuff, Collier and the other Panthers just didn't know how to use it. After more of this discussion, Brown told us, the Panthers drove him and his friend Hayes, unharmed, back to their homes.

The defense lawyers did not seem hostile to Brown; Robert Bloom gently asked him if he recalled the episode clearly—hadn't Collier actually been criticizing Hayes simply for trying to introduce dynamite into the Black Panther Party? Brown wasn't sure whether Collier might have said that, but he did recall the complaint that it hadn't been good stuff.

This episode floated in my recollection as if without visible means of support; without connection. If I did have to contend with the unsavory possibility that the Panthers actually possessed dynamite, I also had to absorb the unsavory possibility that this Roland Hayes, who supposedly admitted to the Panthers that he had been an FBI informer, supplied it; he may have been an agent provocateur. He was never brought before us by either side. Since I was still baffled over the apparent unwillingness of the police to follow Lumumba and his supposed bomb-toting comrades on January 17, Richard Brown's story did not seem worth taking very seriously.

On April 1, in the courtroom, we heard stipulations that Michael Tabor was in Algiers. The DA had actually telephoned him and made tapes of their conversation. I'm sorry that we never heard those. We tried to imagine, "Hello, Mike, this is Joe." "Joe who?" Someone speculated that the DA had timed his call to get the benefit of night rates. And so on. (No one knew where Richard Moore had fled to.)

The witnesses for the defense were not many—ten, as compared with the seventy-odd that the DA had produced. They, however, helped to give us a few clues to the Panthers' lives before the arrests. They also brought out another side of the DA's personality.

The other jurors, I was sure, were as startled as I to hear Phillips suddenly lashing out at a pleasant, slim, alert young white man named Colin Connery. This witness had obviously upset the DA by telling defense lawyers and the jury that the three "pipe bombs" in

Robert Collier's apartment came from a whole basketful
of discarded pieces of plumbing that Collier was using
to install a shower. The pieces had come from the
Tompkins Square Community Center, on the lower
East Side not far from the Colliers' apartment. Connery
said he had worked with Collier at the center, and helped
him and another man put the shower in, at Collier's home.
The three six-inch lengths of pipe were remnants of that
project; the Colliers' daughter had probably played with
them.

Since Connery was a defense witness, it was the
DA who cross-examined this time. "Did you ever see
her playing with a pipe with a jagged edge?" he asked.

"No," Connery said, "I wasn't concerned. If she
were, I think I would have been concerned."

"You would have taken them away from her?"

"I probably would have, yes . . . I might have
overlooked it, too."

"You weren't the child's mother?"

That last remark, as I see it typed out in the court
transcript, makes me do a double-take—what? what?
Some misguided form of sarcasm? What tender spots in
our minds did the DA think he was touching? Counselor Crain objected to the question, and the Judge, to
my surprise, overruled him.

Well, Collier still could have rigged the pipes as
bombs; they did have caps screwed on at each end when
we saw them, and at least one cap on each pipe had a
small hole drilled through the center, suitable for a fuse.
The assembled objects, as Phillips pointed out later,

looked exactly like a pipe bomb illustrated in one of the books on explosives that were in evidence. And there *was* supposed to have been a can of gunpowder on a shelf in the Collier bathroom, though the police testimony on this seemed shaky; Colin Connery and another defense witness told us they never saw it in the apartment.

Connery told us at one point that he had never been arrested and convicted, and that at one time he had shared an apartment with another man in Greenwich Village. The DA asked him for more details about the apartment-sharing; surely, I said to myself, Phillips isn't going to hint at sexual deviation in an attempt to win our minds. If the DA had such intentions, Connery apparently defused them by explaining that the apartment belonged to a Presbyterian minister who had given him living space for a few weeks when he had no other. Would the prosecutor dare to make insinuations about a minister?

Lunchtime came during the cross-examination, so we had a respite from Phillips's snarling tones and emotional implications, his shaking the "pipe bomb" almost in Connery's face, his harsh interruptions which the Judge did not criticize until one of the defense people requested it.

The DA apparently used his lunch hour to check up on Connery; when we reconvened, he asked whether Connery hadn't been arrested once in Chester, Pennsylvania, in 1965. Connery's answer sounded suspicious; he wasn't sure, he might have been. The DA had evidently caught him in a mistake, or a lie—depending on your interpretation.

Connery's other answers were often imprecise, as he tried to explain circumstances about the jobs he had held, the schooling he had received. The DA capitalized on Connery's need to clarify his remarks, and often interrupted when it was obvious that the witness still had something to say. More than once Bloom objected to this, and the Judge had to sustain the objection, but the DA would repeat his interruption anyway. The Judge saw fit to berate—not Phillips, but Bloom: "Counselor, if it weren't for the manner in which you present the issue to the Court, you would get more advantage."

A little later, though, I had the impression that His Honor may have remembered that this was all going on the record, and that we were noticing, because he seemed, reluctantly, to admit that Phillips was getting out of hand. "Mr. Phillips, you are interrupting the witness," he said at last.

Whether Phillips was blowing his cool in the face of his young unflapped witness—and in the flurry of objections from all the lawyers as well as Afeni, along with outbursts from other defendants—or whether crude harassment was part of his technique I couldn't be sure. We all had to sit, as usual, calmly attending.

Phillips said, "Do you know anybody who is a Black Panther?"

"I do now, yes." said Connery.

Crain stood up. "Objection, Your Honor." Because the question, evidently, was out of order.

The Judge said, "Sustained," but the DA carried on: "Who do you know now?"

Bloom stood up. "Objection. It was sustained." He didn't show half the indignation I was feeling.

Phillips said, "I am sorry," and Bloom, hinting that a ruling in favor of the defense was unexpected said, "Mr. Phillips assumed it was not sustained?"

At which the Judge, to my chagrin, said, "The record will reflect that the manner in which Counselor Bloom made that objection was conducive to disorder in this courtroom, and he is admonished to refrain from that kind of conduct."

"May I ask Your Honor," said Bloom, "to specify the manner, please, the conduct."

Judge Murtagh, whose finest moment this was not, said, "Abrupt, showing menace, and creating a disturbance generally by intemperate conduct."

Showing menace? I said to myself.

Afeni stood up. "May I—"

Katz also. "This can't go unanswered, a gratuitous comment that really has no basis in fact. . . ."

The DA soon finished. Bloom said, "I believe I have a few questions, Your Honor. May we have a brief recess? It's 3:15." I suppose he wanted to look into the matter of Connery's "conviction" that the DA had brought up.

Phillips said, "Your Honor, I would object to a brief recess. If there is going to be a redirect, let's have it now."

Afeni announced, "I have to go to the bathroom,"

and the Judge gave us a break.

I couldn't tell how calculated Afeni's remark had been. At any rate, after the recess Bloom asked Connery to explain his arrest.

Connery's bright prominent eyes showed no dismay, no repentance, as he told us about a demonstration that had been held in Chester in 1965 against de facto school segregation. He was enrolled at Swarthmore at the time. He didn't think he wanted to march, so he was hanging around two blocks away when a police van came down the street, full of people who had been arrested. Connery told us he heard one of the policemen say, "There's another one of those mother-fuckers," and he was arrested and taken with the others. They spent a week sleeping on army-surplus cots and eating foul baloney sandwiches. Then they were released, and a lawyer took over the case. The lawyer may have pleaded guilty on some minor charge and paid a fine on the group's behalf, Connery said; he didn't know.

I don't think Phillips comprehended the admiration we all must have felt for Connery at the end of his story. Obviously our deadpans were working well, because he continued to act as if he assumed we were Proper Folk tied to the old traditions. Phillips sneered at another witness, who hadn't gotten along in the air force and was dismissed after he failed to satisfy a psychiatrist who asked him to name one of the astronauts.

A chubby young white woman, Curtis Powell's free-lance photographer friend Roz Payne, caused a little confusion over her name. The DA asked whether she was Mrs. or Miss. She said she had given her married name. "How long have you been using that name?" the DA asked, insinuating God knows what. As Lefcourt faintly objected to the question, Afeni was laughing. The Judge asked counsel to admonish defendants to behave themselves. Afeni, still convulsed, said, "Don't ask me to do anything, 'cause if it's funny, I'm gonna laugh!" Miss/Mrs. Payne was on the stand to tell us that she saw the messed-up condition of Powell's apartment after the police had broken into it. Powell hadn't been there to let them in. Later that day, hearing about the indictment, he had gone to the apartment, where he knew the police were waiting for him. He took Miss/Mrs. Payne along. The defense passed her photographs to us, showing that someone had indeed ransacked the place. Fred said to me, "You see, they move into a nice neighborhood and ruin it." I said, "Yeah, I wonder what the jail looks like by now."

When Joan Bird's mother took the stand the DA was more careful, I thought; you dasn't impugn motherhood. She told us that four men, detectives and policemen, came to her apartment around 3:00 A.M. on January 18—several hours after her daughter was taken on the Harlem River Drive as a "material witness." Mrs. Bird said that Detective Scotty Watson was not at the station when she got there, and that she did not go up to Joan (as Watson had said) to bawl her out for getting into trouble. She said that when Patrolman McKenzie at one point took Joan into a room and shut the door, she could hear Joan screaming. Mrs. Bird's story was at odds with the police stories; I thought, other things being very unequal, at this stage I'll opt for her version. But again, it didn't matter as far as my verdict was concerned. What mattered was the chance to hear someone else from the defense side showing signs of spunky valorous life trying to assert itself against the prosecutor's attacks.

Mrs. Bird, a small, handsome woman wearing dark glasses, with a slight Jamaica bounce in her voice, looked over at us boldly as she spoke. I had greeted her once or twice outside the courtroom and she had said, "How are you this morning?" or something like that. I was surprised to find her so outspoken in the courtroom; sassy. "I will ask the Judge to ask Mr. Phillips, the District Attorney, not to raise his voice at me, because I am not here to be hollered at"—even though the DA's questions had been relatively subdued. When Phillips was asking her about Joan's Panther friends, he said, "Isn't it a fact you met the undercover policeman in this particular case, Mrs. Bird?" and she replied, "Which one? You have so many, maybe you could tell me." He seemed suspicious about Joan's claim to have attended nursing school in the Bronx, and asked about her address. Mrs. Bird said, "Do you know what part of Bronx Community College Joan was going to?"

"I know exactly, Mrs. Bird."

"I guess you do."

Shirley Jones also appeared, obviously as reluctant as she claimed to be. Lefcourt had sent her a subpoena, we learned, after several attempts to persuade her to

come on her own volition; Phillips claimed that the subpoena wasn't valid. This former friend of Ralph White,
an exotic-looking black woman in a white turban, told
us that she had frequently seen the back room of the
Elsmere Tenants Council when she visited the place,
and that the famous tabletops had been leaning against
the rear wall, not at all toward the refrigerator room.
She gave a few other details about the place that didn't
match White's. The DA went relatively easy on her;
after all, she presumably knew a great deal about one of
his major spies. Neither he nor the defense asked at any
length about her relationship with White.

Phillips was also refreshingly deferential to a short
man—he reminded me of Alan Ladd—who had been
Clark Squire's boss and verified that Squire had been
getting a salary of $17,000 a year. He said that his com-
pany, which was involved with computers, had no dangerous chemicals. (Squire, supposedly, during the conspiracy had said he would get explosive chemicals where
he worked.) Phillips asked the man if there were any
firms in the same building—in midtown Manhattan—
where chemicals could be obtained. The man didn't
know.

After one or two other minor witnesses, we realized
that we had completed another phase. On April 14,
Wednesday, the prosecution and the defense "rested."
Each defense lawyer rose and spoke the formula—
Gerald Lefcourt rested for Lumumba Shakur and Rich-
ard Moore; Carol Lefcourt for Walter Johnson; William
Crain for Ali Bey Hassan; Sanford Katz for Lee Roper

and Joan Bird; Robert Bloom for Robert Collier, Curtis Powell, and Alex McKeiver; Charles McKinney for William King and Clark Squire.

The DA said that there was one more party to be heard from. Afeni stood and said, "I rest."

"*I* rest," said Bowser behind me.

"I rest," said Butters.

The DA smiled.

"Why Are We Here?"

Since the defense lawyers had to do their summations first, they were at a disadvantage, as they told us, having to anticipate what Phillips would say. He would be able to comment on their statements, but they would have to remain largely silent after they finished.

Two bright things about the summations—besides their signaling the approach of the end—were that they permitted each side to make comments about the other's case in terms that weren't proper during the presentation of evidence and testimony and cross-examination: and they gave the lawyers a chance to point out corroborations or discrepancies that we might have missed. "I guess they can say anything they want now," somebody remarked in the jury room after Katz had started the first summation. Not *quite* true.

Each lawyer, concentrating on the defendants assigned to him/her, gave us a version of the DA's case and the arguments against it. Each one ended with an eloquent plea for the defendants' freedom. Sanford Katz, the most noticeably angry of the six defenders, took the greater part of one day. He reminded us of Gene Roberts's story about the Shell road map on which defendant King had supposedly marked sections of the New Haven Railroad that were to be blown up. A map that didn't even indicate railroad lines; sites like Spuyten Duyvil, that the railroad didn't go near. Never mind whose absurdity it was, I thought—Roberts's or King's; the indictments on this charge were among the silliest of all. Katz ended by pointing to the large windows above and behind us, filled with the sunshine that, as he said, had been kept from most of the defendants for two years. As we were going home in the afternoon, Butters said something about being moved by that conclusion. I didn't hear his entire remark, and wasn't sure whether he was using Katzian sarcasm.

In my journal I wrote, "Katz is refreshingly free of jury-flattering, except by dry implication. I wonder if the DA will try cozening." Little did I know.

William Crain, who spoke the next day, was less dry, sometimes repetitious and overly rhetorical. "That was what was going on that day. That was what was going on that day." "But let's go further. Let's go further." He gave us his judgments of the evidence and testimony in large generalities before telling us the specifics. During a break, in the men's room I was softly complaining to someone that Crain might be consuming more time than was necessary, and Fox made a lively defense: "That's just the way he is, man."

Crain did show us plenty of facts, contradictions, incompletenesses, absurdities. About the rifle and ammunition found in the red car near the Harlem River Drive: "When you go hunting and you have bought four boxes of shells [as had been indicated somewhere along the line], do you go hunting with five bullets, when you have a whole car to store the extras in?" I didn't blame him, as he spoke before our blank faces, for feeling that he had to underline and overcolor his points; how could he be sure that the facts themselves were working on us?

Carol Lefcourt spoke on behalf of Baba Odinga (Walter Johnson). She was more forceful than usual, and she didn't take long; there wasn't much, she said, to implicate her client. She ended, "So I will leave in your hands the life of Baba Odinga," and I had to suppress the jolt I felt.

That was April 26; in the evening I wrote:

As we file out, McKinney looks up at each of us as we pass. I would give him an encouraging look if it weren't for the officers and other court types sitting nearby. Jesus—watching and waiting and wondering; sweating it out. But I am also in my small way sweating it out, afraid that one or two—it wouldn't take more than one—of the jurors will louse things up, force a miserable compromise of some kind.

Robert Bloom followed Mrs. Lefcourt, with remarks about the DA's enormous power, including the power to select the judge to preside in this case. At which His Honor declared a brief recess, and we marched out and waited while Bloom, we guessed, got some kind of what-for. It was brief; we were soon called back and sat down. Bloom said, "May I proceed, Your Honor?" and Miss Yanes said a loud "No," because it

turned out that Gary was not with us. We waited while
an officer went to fetch him. Gary had been in the men's
room when we were summoned, and a Court officer had,
as usual, locked the jury room door.

Bloom made a few comments that especially im-
pressed me, about the grand jury that had brought the
indictment—the second one, in October 1969. Twenty-
three people, not chosen by both sides, not able to hear
any defense reply to the charges, not needing more
than a majority to decide on indicting the Panthers.
These comments brought closer to my surface the sub-
terranean rumblings in my soul. Likewise, the bright
compassionate unphony quality of all the unpaid defense
lawyers. Fair trial? After two years in prison? And by
what stroke of luck did these impoverished prisoners
happen to have such a high-grade roster of attorneys?

But I wrote in my journal:

*Of course I have to reserve judgment until I hear
the DA; and even at this stage I can honestly say that I
frankly sincerely patriotically dutifully think that it is
faintly possible that he will pull all his bits and pieces together into a sharp picture of conspiracy. Maybe there
is something big there that has escaped my busy mind.
There must be something that enables him to believe,
still, that he has a case.*

The Muse of Eloquence and Contradiction nudged
me:

*Yes—those fluorescent bits of phony dynamite—
linked by what miracle of imagination to all defendants?*

Shine on, oatmeal and clay, prove to us that this disreputable miscellaneous bunch of blacks are criminals, because if you don't you can join the rotting bodies of the My Lai victims (those corpses may be fluorescing * *too, now) as more signals that America is slipping into her own shit.*

Bloom's voice grew weak around 4:15; he asked the Judge if we could break for the day. His Honor was reluctant; the trial, he pointed out, had already taken a very long time. He had made such remarks before, and always seemed to imply that the lengthiness was the defense's fault—one of the most unconscionable remarks, I thought, in the course of this unconscionable trial. But the Judge did grant the break.

It was a relief for us, too. As I left the building with Miss Yanes she made one of the first judgments I had heard from her—about how she admired Bloom. She also agreed with me that it was good to be reminded of things we might have forgotten, and to have many of the details put together at last—as the lawyers set some observations made by Roberts in November, for example, against testimony that we heard from Ashwood in March.

Bloom reminded us the next day of the three bottles of chemicals the police had found at Curtis Powell's apartment. None of them was especially useful in concocting bombs, but one was a powerful poison, and the others *could* be used for explosives with a great deal of

* I meant "phosphorescing."

manipulation, and with other ingredients. But Bloom asked us to recall that two other bottles had also been found at Powell's place. The prosecution's chemical expert, a genial, homely policeman who directed his comments down to the Court reporter, had told us that when he received the five bottles he set two of them aside, because he knew they had nothing to do with explosives. Bloom had asked him whether they contained liquid. Yes, said the police expert. Could the liquid have been rat urine? Yes. Powell had worked at Delafield Institute, supposedly in cancer research, we had heard. The chemicals and rat urine (or whatever it was) seemed to have little to do with bombing department stores or railroad yards or anything. The bottles of urine—which could have been what I call counterevidence—were excluded by the police chemist, under who knows what orders or personal impulse?

Both Bloom and Crain mentioned a curious circumstance about some of the debris collected by police after the mini-explosion at the Forty-fourth Precinct station. I remembered that three of the small brown envelopes that we handled had contained pieces of broken glass from the dirty windows of the station (actually, as I recalled, one of the envelopes was empty). The fourth had contained the crumbs of debris that partly fluoresced under the ultraviolet light; it was dated a day or two later than the others. Had some ingenious policeman planted the fluorescent stuff, strewn it around the place, to be discovered by detectives? I easily believed that it was possible.

There were two forces represented in the court-room battle, Bloom said. "These are political people, not criminals."

Phillips broke in: "Your Honor, counsel is summing up facts outside the record."

Afeni started to speak, and the Judge said, "Please, Mrs. Shakur, be seated. I direct you to be seated."

"I direct you to leave me alone," said Afeni.

The other force, Bloom went on to say, was John Mitchell, J. Edgar Hoover, and so on. "The jury is the last line of protection for the defendants here on trial. . . . Indeed, ladies and gentlemen, you are the last word. Nobody can overrule you. Nobody can hold you in contempt, and nobody can silence you if you say these defendants are innocent." He finished by asking us to be fair, to "take your places in the history of freedom."

In my notes for April 27:

I've been telling jurors that if they want to get together right after the verdict, to talk it all over safe from any reporters who might be interested, they can come here to my place. But I wonder if I'll feel so friendly then.

Next came Gerald Lefcourt; terse, direct, clear. Like the others, he spoke from a dauntingly thick pad of notes. His were typed. He read from them a great deal, but not always. One of his interesting psychological points was that Ralph White seemed an unstable man

who may have been so avid for praise from his superiors
that he began to exaggerate and invent details about
Lumumba, dynamite, and other things that were to im-
press the grand jury.

The DA interrupted at one point to ask for some
legal citation, and Katz spoke up to protest Phillips's
"shyster tactics."

The Judge said, "I ask you, Counselor Katz, to be
seated."

At which we heard Joan Bird's voice for the first
time—sharp and angry: "Stop badgering my lawyer!"

"Your lawyer is out of order," said the Judge.

"So are you," said Joan.

Lefcourt, like Bloom, reminded us that the jury is
accountable to no one. "I think . . . the government
has declared war on these people, and you, the jury, are
the only thing that separates the government from them.
You have the ultimate power here, and nobody—nobody—can review it."

Except for that faint possibility that the DA might
offer some unforeseen revelation—which I may have
cherished as a small counterbalance to anger—it seemed
that my decision had by then pretty well made itself. So,
for about seven months, I had obeyed His Honor's in-
struction that we presume the defendants innocent until proven guilty.

Lefcourt's call to us to understand the total power
we had was stirring and upsetting. He ended his eloquent crisp summation about 3:00 P.M. There was a
break. Again we didn't get much of a respite; after a

few minutes the Court officers called us back in. As we
passed through the door Obie Tunstall said, "We ought
to get a shoe allowance."

After we sat down, Afeni Shakur came over to
speak to us. Tough young Afeni was very pregnant,
very weary, her voice trembling from either emotion or
her bad cough. Her eyes seemed to be wet, but I thought
that, too, might be from her cold. I wanted to think it,
because I didn't want sentimentality, or sentiment even,
to reach me there and then.

"I have very little to say, because it has all been
said. . . . Forgive me if I stray from legal jargon, for I
am not a lawyer. I have chosen to defend myself, against
the advise of cocounsel, the Court, friends; as a matter of
fact, against my own intellect, whatever that is. I do it
now, as I have in the past, because I know better than
any lawyer in America that Afeni Shakur is not guilty
of the charges before you.

"No one can say more vehemently that Afeni is
innocent than Afeni herself. So here I am—scared, shaking, nervous, but full of the knowledge that I cannot beg
you for pity. There is no need for that."

The spectators and reporters were listening closely.
The jurors were listening closely.

"I am tired. I am tired. I am sick. I am sick of all
this. . . . I do know that none of those charges have
been proven, and I'm not talking about proving beyond
a reasonable doubt. I'm saying that those charges have
not been proven, period. . . ."

She quoted parts of the transcript in which Roberts,

White, and Ashwood said they hadn't seen any specific crimes committed. "So then why are we here? Why are any of us here? I don't know. But I would appreciate it if you would end this nightmare, because I'm tired of it, and I can't justify it in my mind. There's no logical reason for us to have gone through the last two years as we have, to be threatened with imprisonment because somebody somewhere is watching and waiting to justify his being a spy. . . . Please don't forget what you saw and heard in this courtroom. Don't forget any of it; this extravaganza has already found its place among the Oscar winners.

"Let history record you as a jury who would not kneel to the outrageous bidding of the state. Justify our faith in you. . . . Show us that we were not wrong in assuming that you would judge us fairly. . . . Please judge us according to the way you want to be judged.

"That's all I have to say."

A spectator said in a low voice, "Right on."

The next day the Judge sent us away because two defendants—King and Powell—were sick. I said, "We should have alternate defendants." I went to a coffee shop with Joe and Claudette; we talked about the emotional effect of Afeni's speech—an impact that hardly anyone could deny. Claudette said she was not sorry to have this one-day vacation; she'd been so drained by the speech that she felt she had to level off. We talked about racism, law and order, the dangers of being radical, the buildings burning in black Brooklyn slums. Claudette said something that surprised me: she might have been persuaded to be a Black Panther, but if she had, she would have taken care to do nothing illegal to get herself arrested. Joe and I raised eyebrows, probably both wanting to ask, "Do you think that would have protected you?" She went on to say she was sure there was a dossier on her, on all of us; we didn't disagree with that.

Charles McKinney gave the last defense summation, ushering us into May. He had only three or four sheets of notes, so most of his speech was extemporaneous. It lasted for about an hour. As he reminded us that there were no witnesses to corroborate the spies' stories—despite the usually large numbers of Panthers who attended the gatherings—he repeated several times a kind of chorus: "Does not this raise a reasonable doubt? I suggest that it does."

I wrote in my journal:

He ended up most obviously eloquent—beautiful. We should go down all eighteen charges [as the number stood then] against each and every one of the thirteen defendants, and find each and every defendant not guilty. Yes, he said, we'll be criticized afterward, but by finding them all not guilty we will help to preserve the honor of New York State.

As he finished there were, for the first time, outright applause and cheering and cries of "Right on!"

What were the other jurors thinking?

The cheering wasn't stifled; the guards did nothing, as far as I could see, except walk into the aisles. The excitement soon subsided and the Judge made a perfunctory remark that demonstrations would not be allowed in the courtroom.

The Age of Cool may be waiting in the wings.

Is there still time for it?

As I typed my notes at intervals that evening in my apartment, I brooded over this culmination. I was not logically ticking off evidence and counterevidence; I was in an emotional stew, a kind of baffled despair. It didn't matter that the defendants, some of that diverse bunch, may have had unlovely records. They hadn't conspired to commit all those crimes, we had heard no proof at all that they had done any of the things that the mysterious grand juries had accused them of. When I wasn't typing notes, I was listening to records. Jefferson Airplane, "Wooden Ships." Janis Joplin singing "Me and Bobby McGee." Odetta doing her superb slow version of Bob Dylan's "Mr. Tambourine Man"—"I am ready to go anywhere, I am ready for to fade into my own parade." With some Ives or Bach or Buxtehude. I had an imageless shuddering sense of the Establishment, the System, a machine grinding forward to crush the victim, scrunch. I wrote:

Midnight nearly.

Joys of music and horrors of thought. Way down. When you think about what man does to man, the nails through your hands don't matter. Way down, thrillingly down. Only for an instant. Eli, Eli, lama sabacthani.

And the beautiful kids in Washington today, trying to tie up traffic, kept those cops and soldiers busy!

Gorgeous days of disaster.

Father Joe

The prosecution spoke to us next. Mr. Phillips of the bright, large, pleasant face and glittering blue eyes. Dressed in a plain black suit, including vest, with a white shirt, and a blue tie only slightly striped with color; like a genial priest. Father Joe explaining dogma to the parishioners.

Lefcourt had predicted in his summation that the DA would make special preparations; to our right, now, was a large display rack with five rifles (one a carbine), seven pistols—handguns anyhow. On each of them hung a tag lettered "Tabor," "Moore," and so on. Walking toward the jury room that morning I had seen the rack through the open courtroom door. I asked Hiram if he noticed it. He laughed and said, "Yes—I'm not going in there!"

Young Jeffrey Weinstein continued to sit at Phillips's table, holding up the familiar articles of evidence as Phillips needed them, from a wide spread of overlapping brown envelopes, bottles, "pipe bombs," coil of fuse wire. I saw as we filed in that Phillips had the white Santa Claus bag, with Eddie Joseph's aerosol cans, stashed under the Court reporter's little table.

Phillips, of course, winding up what he said was the longest trial in the history of New York State, went over nearly all the statements and objects that he had offered to us during the endless months. He told us at the start of his speech, "I promise that we won't be any more than a day and a half. So that we should finish, I would think, by Wednesday, the People's summation." That was Tuesday, May 4; he finished on the following Tuesday, May 11. But we had the usual Friday off, and there were delays and interruptions—we missed Thursday afternoon because Ben Giles got sick—so Phillips really spoke not much more than twice as long as he had promised. It was grueling; I dreaded trying to go through that long weekend, days of blank. I don't know why his summation expanded itself so generously; maybe he felt that he wasn't getting to us.

He tried hard enough. He joked with us, alluded to each juror personally in one way or another, kept saying, "You remember that, don't you?" as he reiterated details of the trial. He interlocked his knuckles to show us how the evidence meshed to prove his case. "It fits like the gears in a car, the gears in a machine." All the little things he was recounting for us would establish the criminal acts that these crude people with their "uneducated minds" were up to. His appeals to our recollection, like his quips, were supposed to generate some kind of response in our faces; we were supposed to smile or nod our heads. But we sat like stones. At one point Weinstein interrupted to correct him on a small matter and Phillips said, "The man who should be summing up in this case is Mr. Weinstein, because he is much more effective than I am." It was a lodge-meeting pleasantry, the kind that is not meant to be taken seriously but is meant to be laughed at because we all belong to the same club, share the same assumptions. We didn't laugh. To explain some of the mistakes his witnesses had made, Phillips said that everyone makes slips of the lip—even the Judge had, once or twice; but a police officer, he said, isn't forgiven, "He becomes the worst guy in the world if he made a slip of the lip. . . ." He looked at us for sympathy. "It is enough to make you ill."

Cajoling, coddling, cozening. During a break I said to Nils, "And they told us this wouldn't be like television trials." At one point Weinstein suggested to Phillips that we ask for a recess. The DA looked at us and said, "How about a break? Seconded?" Nobody said a word or moved a muscle, as far as I could tell. "No?" said Phillips. The Judge started to call a recess, but Steve had begun to make a churning motion with his hand and said, "Let's go on," and a couple of us murmured yes. So okay, okay, we went on.

I've always found it difficult to keep from smiling or laughing out of politeness when some genial person is trying to make a joke. So I had to stop looking at Phillips; I stared over at Weinstein, remarkably handsome in his trim suit, at Phillips's hands or necktie, at the defendants and their lawyers—Bloom's face smiling beyond Phillips's left elbow. I did laugh at one point when Phillips paused in his speech and again asked if we wanted a break; we said nothing, but Weinstein said, "*I do.*" His Honor granted one.

And there were occasional waves of courtroom titters, as when Phillips was insisting that the dynamite had been real, not a figment of Ralph White's brain—after all that corroboration. "If that's not true," he said, "then nothing is true in this case." That was one of my finest moments of straight-face. Another of Phillips's comments—maybe it was his explanation that he hadn't brought the other police spy to the witness stand because "that would have made it a nine-month trial instead of seven months"—struck me as so absurd that I must have made a face or squirmed or something; I turned my eyes toward the spectators inadvertently, and a young woman in the front row saw this and smiled. Then I looked toward Bloom, and I thought he must have noticed. I quickly tried to gather my features into a blank.

The DA went on, trying to tighten up his meshing gears. "The fanatics are at work." He reminded us of "the December thirty-first call-box attack." He talked about a piece of evidence that we had never examined, a paper from the files of the New York City Transit Authority indicating that William King did not report for his subway-booth job on January 17, 1969. This slippery gear-mesh he put into full speed: the file, he said, "shows that King took the day off from work in order to participate in this case. . . . You find corroboration of where King was on the January seventeenth date." I tried to imagine a subway supervisor filling in the space on King's file: "Absent, delivering dynamite to police station."

Even Phillips had frivolous moments—"And you recall the cross-examination about whether it was a Baggie or a plastic wrapper from a Marlboro pack"— referring to Ralph White's story of how Mshina wrapped a dynamite cap. "And, really, what's the difference?"

One day at lunch Nils went so far as to say of Phillips, "He simply doesn't know the audience he's talking to." Joe and Claudette agreed. But Nils also said something general about the jury's having to sort out valid points from invalid ones, and I had to keep from blurting, "What valid points?" We went on to talk of other things—the section of Brooklyn that was on fire; the "monetary disturbance" caused by Germany when she devalued our dollar; the citizens of Washington, D.C., who were angry because the war protesters were tying up traffic. Then we went back to complaining about the length of Phillips's speech; we could judge roughly from his chronology that he had some time to go yet. I said, joking, "I wish some of us *would* say, 'Yes, we remember, we remember,' when he asks us. That might speed him up."

That Friday I had to go to the office, and the work kept my mind occupied. But on Saturday and Sunday I was at loose ends. I felt spiritless, dull; apprehensive; anxious; impatient. I said to myself, Multiply these feelings by those of the eleven defendants and six lawyers. And the other jurors? And the Judge? I even imagined that Jeffrey Weinstein might share them, and wondered if he hadn't been sitting in the courtroom thinking, *Hopeless, hopeless.*

I thought of trying to lose myself by reading about Alice, chasing her through the looking glass, maybe followed by Patrolman McKenzie with his pierced summons pouch, Ralph White with his fluorescent fingers, Gene Roberts with his electronic breast, Carlos Ashwood with his blank eyes, Scotty Watson with his hearty confessional compassion—we would all fall down the rabbit hole and feed our heads with Dr. Curtis Powell's colorful chemicals and try to keep from drowning in Alice's tears. With guns and bullets and fuse wire floating around us, we would dance and drown while Afeni and Lumumba and Dharuba and Cetewayo and Baba and Ali Bey and Katara and Squire sneaked through the back door of Rockland Palace to go underground once again in their headquarters and apartments and schools and streets.

This sober-wild trip (I was not stoned on anything but anger) shook me hard as I remembered that Afeni's "slave name," the name she was given at birth, was Alice Williams.

Phillips continued on Monday. He tried to answer many of the defense attorneys' points, but said nothing about the toilet room that Ralph White had belatedly remembered between refrigerator and tabletops at the Elsmere Tenants Council. He did recall for us the night that Gene Roberts and three Panthers drove to Baltimore for a gun and ammunition. "As Mr. Chaberski pointed out, that clip in the weapon had ceremonials—"

"Empty blanks," said Steve out loud.

Phillips acknowledged this, but misunderstood. "—blank ammunition in it. And that's a good point. . . . If the police were planting anything to frame anybody, they wouldn't use blanks, as Mr. Chaberski pointed out."

That wasn't what Steve had had in mind, and, as he mentioned to me later, it wasn't about that episode that Steve had raised the question of empty blanks, it was a gun seized in Michael Tabor's apartment. On top of it all, Steve reminded me, the bullets weren't even "ceremonials" because they had no powder in them at all.

To answer the objection that the Panthers never talked about an Easter plot during that entire midnight-to-morning excursion a week before Easter, Phillips said that they were probably too tired to talk. I said to myself, "Oh."

The curious fact that some items of evidence found in the defendants' apartments were in plain view—especially when the police didn't happen to have a search warrant—didn't seem unanswerable to the DA. The revolver that a cop had spotted on a headboard over Alex McKeiver's bed—"I think Mr. Bloom on his cross-examination suggested that the police put it there. Mr. Bloom's clients are always the clients where we take guns and we put them under headboards, where we take—"

"Objection," said Bloom, asking the DA to cite the

page of the transcript where he had made the suggestion.

Judge: "Objection overrruled. . . ."

The obliging DA: "3758."

Afeni: "That man is crazy!"

Judge: "I'll ask Mrs. Shakur to behave herself, or we will have to excuse her from the courtroom."

And we rolled on. When Crain interrupted once with "He is not arguing from the evidence, Your Honor," the Judge said, "Apparently he is doing too well for you. Be seated."

Phillips got to me once; he was explaining why the spy witnesses had to use their reports so often to refresh their recollection. He seemed to be far from calm. "If I asked you, 'What about February 8th,' and you say, 'Let me look at the record, and I will tell you.' . . . But if I didn't want the answer, if I wanted to confuse you, if I wanted to take advantage of you, then I would say, 'Not now, Mr. Kennebeck. I am not going to give you your reports now. . . .' and I harass you for a while about what happened on February 8th, and 'Didn't you say this on February 8th?' . . . and you really can't recall February 8th. . . . *That* is how you can be misled. *That* is how you can be confused." I know I flushed as he shook his finger and aimed his words at me. I know I didn't look him in the eye, as I probably should have. Yeah, he could get me rattled on a witness stand.

When he showed us the handcuffs that were found in Richard Moore's apartment, he looked at Joe and said he was sure Mr. Rainato would remember them. Ha ha.

But Joe reminded me afterward that the cuffs he got involved with the pair that Tabor was said to have owned.

Phillips pointed to his display rack and ran down the names of the various gun owners. At recess time, Hiram told me the DA had pointed to the same gun for both Lee Roper (captured in Cleveland) and Curtis Powell. A couple of other jurors noticed the mistake, understandable enough in the welter of Phillips's premises and conclusions.

As he was reviewing the arrests, he reminded us of the policeman on a roof near Walter Johnson's place who saw the leg emerging from Johnson's window and threatened to blow it off. I noticed a middle-aged black woman get up from her seat in the audience and walk out, muttering. It was Walter Johnson's mother. Later she returned to her seat next to Joan Bird's mother. Bearing the face of grief.

Phillips tried to weave us all in. Talking about some Panther forays into the Brox Botanical Garden in mid-March, he said that it was a cold season, there was usually snow in the Adirondacks in mid-March. This was a pointless allusion to a Monday when we had to have a court recess because Jim Butters was snowed in after a weekend upstate. Phillips, in his comments on the tape recordings that we had heard, with the typed script, said he was sure Fred Hills would remember one particular conversation because he had asked to have that page replayed. Fred didn't look at him or smile. I whispered, "You were probably asleep."

The DA tried to cajole us by implying that the cops had been nice enough not to shoot those armed dangerous criminals on April 2 when they arrested them. He said something that Crain broke into with an objection, at which Phillips hollered, "Look at the faker now!" Crain asked the Judge to admonish Phillips, and Phillips apologized.

He even did a little scenario in which he enlisted Fox, Beiser, Chaberski, Rainato, Weinstein, and himself. They were to plot the robbery of "a very, very good liquor store." Fox was the master mind, Steve the lookout, and so on. This was by way of showing how several people can be involved in a criminal conspiracy without all knowing the complete plan, or even each other. As usual, the jury response was not playful cooperation but discomfort.

I had lunch that day at Chi Mer with Joe, Nils, and Butters. As we walked across the park behind the courthouse on the way to Chinatown, Butters said, "Charlie Bowser says the deliberation will take five minutes." I said, "Bullshit, it'll take six." My way of mixing wishful thinking with jokey anxiety.

In the late afternoon on Monday, as Joe and I left the building to walk over to the subway, we saw Afeni getting into a cab with Carol Lefcourt. Afeni and Joan had both been socked back in jail after Tabor and Moore split in February—they were in the Women's House of Detention on West Tenth Street, a few blocks from where I live, and I sometimes walked past that hard place in the evening—but now Judge Murtagh had let

Afeni out because of her pregnancy. As Joe and I went on across the street I looked back at the defendant and the lawyer, for some reason wanting to greet them, and to be greeted. They didn't notice. I wondered whether Afeni at that point would be tempted to abuse her freedom. I imagined her thinking: Maybe this week I'll be found guilty, sentenced; maybe the baby will be born in jail, or under guard.

On Tuesday, May 11, the DA concluded around noon, after giving us a nearly tearful account of the two policemen who risked their lives in the Harlem River Drive shoot-out. Naturally, he said, the atmosphere that night was tense at the precinct station where they took Joan Bird. These men had had a close shave, almost had to worry about who would take care of their wives and children. Father Joe's voice almost shook. Was he trying to say, in effect, that we should be able to understand if the two cops did happen to beat a little upside Joan's head?

He reminded us of what we had said under oath at the voir dire—we would weigh the evidence and be willing to discuss it fully with all our fellows, and come up with a fair verdict. He urged us to look again at any evidence that concerned us. We could ask the Court officer for permission to see it; we could have any part of the Court transcript read back to us. I suppose we could have seen *The Battle of Algiers* again if we had wished. I was saying to myself that I'd like to ask for just one item—Ali Bey Hassan's sword cane. I couldn't remember any mention of it in the DA's summation.

Phillips finished by apologizing for the length of his speech, and said he was sure we would bring justice to the trial by convicting the defendants. "Let me just conclude and say thank you very, very much for your attention."

"Looking at You,
Ladies and Gentlemen"

After the DA's words of gratitude it was time for His Honor to summarize the evidence. Steve had told me only a few days earlier that a judge always had to do this, and I was distressed to think of sitting through it all. Hadn't we just heard it summarized, from different points of view, by all the lawyers? I'm sure the Judge didn't enjoy the job; in fact, the quality of his summary made me suspect that he had gone at it with weary reluctance. As Steve had remarked a couple of times in the last weeks, His Honor seemed to want nothing more than to get this trial over with.

So he began after lunch on Tuesday, May 11, and—with his charge to us and other formalities—made a speech that lasted through Thursday morning. For the most part, I got no hints or revelations about how the other jurors were feeling about it—everyone probably just waiting for the whole trial to be finished, finished well, as I was. His summary was a lumpy recollection of prosecution testimony and evidence, from the arresting officers to Ashwood and the few miscellaneous final witnesses. I guessed that His Honor might have used several assistants to write up various parts of the record, condensing it to the highlights. He read monotonously, as I probably would have in his place, going over nearly all the points that we were carrying so vividly in our heads. He got a few of the Panther names wrong. One of the women we had heard about, Ife Balagoon, whose first name was pronounced "Eefay," came from the Judge as "Iffy." When he quoted comments about bombing department stores, he said that some women were to "trip" into the place instead of "tip" in. He showed little interest in or feeling for the talk and manners of these alien people.

When he came to Ralph White and the dynamite he said nothing about the extra room behind the refrigerator; concerning Shirley Jones's damaging remarks on the incident he said only, "She also testified as to the location of the area where certain tabletops were located. . . ." I almost gaped at him; and I think I made an effort not to move my eyes out to the audience.

The Judge: "So much for my recollection of the testimony. I repeat, it is your—" He broke off. "Mr. Katz, will you have the decency to allow me to address the jury uninterrupted?"

"You may do so, sir," said Katz. "I didn't think I was interrupting you."

"Your manners leave a great deal to be desired"— one of the Judge's favorite mild reprimands.

"We are all wondering about the lack of cross-examination that was not explained to the jury."

Tell him, Katz. Joe Rainato later said he heard some of the reporters commenting on the omission as well.

The Judge said, "You are out of order. The Court has presented to the jury its best recollection of the testimony. It admonishes the jury that neither the Court's recollection of the testimony nor counsels' recollection of the testimony should affect your recollection and judgment as to what the evidence is. You and you alone determine what the facts are. . . ."

Yes, Your Honor, I said to myself, but for your *own* sake . . .

Before we left on Wednesday afternoon, Mr. William Wallace, the chief Court officer—large, distinguished-looking black man—had said, "Come prepared tomorrow." Prepared for a hotel sojourn of several days. He said we wouldn't have an opportunity to go home for our things before we started deliberations; if necessary, someone would make a phone call for us to arrange delivery of anything we needed. On the next morning the lined-up spectators waiting to get in saw us pass by with luggage like tourists on the move. I had been wondering, along with the other jurors, what swanky hotel accommodations we might have, what strange exclusive meals, under guard, in restaurants. For months I had relished the sense of privilege that fate had bestowed on us—even our special ride down on the freight elevator at the end of each day.

Judge Murtagh was always eminently polite to us, respectful, of course. Once when we were straggling out of the jury room at lunchtime he happened to emerge from his room just as I was passing his door. We both hesitated and smiled. He said, "I yield to the jury." During his final words to us in the courtroom he said, "Looking at you, ladies and gentlemen, I can see that you regard this as a formidable challenge." And, before finishing, "You deserve special commendation for your extraordinary patience and tolerance in this trial." I took the praise with some feeling of irony. "It has been a long and difficult trial, and you have participated with evident patience and understanding. You are entitled to the gratitude of all the citizens of the community for the sacrifice you have made and for the services you are rendering in the faithful performance of a public duty."

He had reduced the counts from the original thirty —we never did hear them all—to sixteen, and now he proceeded to eliminate a few more. Count eleven, "reckless endangerment," was out—but that, as the DA had told us, was only another way of describing the alleged bombing and shooting attempt on January 17. Count sixteen, cutting police call-box wires on New Year's Eve, was out, by golly. "Criminal mischief" was still in there somewhere. But there was no charge referring strictly and only to possession of guns. The Judge even said, "I am refraining from submitting to you the six so-called pistol counts, charging the possession of a pistol." Six counts concerning one pistol! I didn't understand this extraordinary omission, but I felt no impulse to write him a note about it. The reason for reducing the number of charges, he took some pains to tell us, was "in order to avoid giving you issues of a complexity that would interfere with your ability to reach a fair verdict."

The defense lawyers had anticipated him by trying to make his explanation sound like an insult to our intelligence. But I gathered that many of the charges did overlap, because of legal-technical variations; in law and elsewhere, I suppose, the best way to make sure everything is covered is to overlap even the overlaps.

The most serious charge involved the word "murder." Count number one was the crime of *conspiracy* in the first degree—to commit murder. Number two was the crime of *attempted* murder (on the Harlem River Drive), and the next three were variants of it. We listened to these technicalities with sharp concentration. After all the months—after two years—after newspaper headlines, "Free the Panther 21" protest marches, Tom Wolfe's radical chic article—after District Attorney Hogan's terrible prideful announcements—after the many days of our own lives that had become radically tangled with these historic national tremors, with the roots of American trouble—we were face to face with the lined up, numbered statements that reduced it all to legal words, and twelve of us were about to distill those words into the ultimate minimum, Guilty or Not Guilty.

The Judge explained that the "conspiracy to" and

"attempted" charges were referred to in law as anticipa-
tory or inchoate crimes. Maybe in this trial he feared
that we might be confused over the lack of real-action
crimes. "The word 'inchoate' is a word that refers to
something that has just begun or is incipient"—as con-
trasted with "substantive" crimes (such as cutting call-
box wires?). The technical charge in number six was
"conspiracy in the second degree," *which* consisted of
conspiracy to commit arson in the first degree (in this
case the bombing-burning of police stations and department stores).

It all sounded peculiar and remote, as did count
number seven, which was an *attempt* to commit arson in
the first degree (one of the precinct stations), and what
made it seem even more odd was that this charge evidently took precedence over the next, number eight,
which was the actual crime of arson in the first degree.
And number nine was arson in the second degree. We
learned that first-degree arson is burning or blowing up
a building where there is someone inside, or where there
is strong reason to believe that someone is inside—such
as a police precinct station, which presumably always
has a man on duty. So that, I guessed, was why we once
had on the witness stand a policeman who told us only
that he was on duty at the Twenty-fourth Precinct station on the night of January 17. If the "dynamite" sticks
were tossed into the station's back yard that night, his
presence raised the arson attempt one degree. Second-de-
gree arson, as we justice freshmen learned, is the same
thing without anyone in the building.

Count ten, the DA had explained, was the one that
included "criminal mischief"—it had to do with the
agreement to bomb railway tracks and subways. Since
count eleven was out, along with count twelve (a variant
of number thirteen) and count fourteen (a variant of
fifteen), we had only two more. Number thirteen, possession of weapons and dangerous instruments and appliances on or about January 17, 1969. Number fifteen,
identical except for the date: possession of those things
on April 2, 1969. In other words, to oversimplify a lot,
did Lumumba Shakur have dynamite in January and did
Robert Collier have pipe bombs in April? All the rifles
and revolvers and bullets on the DA's show-window rack
that loomed at our right during his summation had dissolved, like gunsmoke in the breeze.

Just as baffling, to me, were His Honor's instructions about possessing explosive substances. "The law
provides that this possession constitutes *presumptive* evidence that said possession was with the *intent to use* the
same unlawfully against the person or property of
another." The puzzled italics are mine. He explained
further: we can't find someone guilty of possessing
explosives unless we decide that he intended to use them
against someone or his property; but, as Lewis Carroll
might be fascinated to know, the fact that the culprit
possessed the stuff allows us to presume that he intended
to use it criminally. It seemed to me to be a sticky
roundabout: a viscous circle? I wondered whether our
presumption couldn't cover the possibility that the culprit might have collected some gunpowder or dynamite

(or firecrackers?) just to show off with, or to use for a lesson in demolition.

Around noon on Thursday the Judge said, "Before I formally submit the case to you . . . I will declare a brief recess." As we got up, I checked Nils Rasmussen's seat and saw that the wad of gum was still stuck underneath. Historical continuity okay. It wasn't lunchtime yet. When we had first come in that wet morning, with our suitcases and satchels, a Court officer asked us to make a list of our sandwich and beverage requests for lunch. I think there was supposed to be a limit to the cost, but nobody gave it much thought. We asked for Cokes and coffee and such; Bill Beiser ordered beer.

I had brought a ham-and-cheese sandwich from home, which I shared with Claudette. We sat around for a long while, nearly an hour. "What are they doing out there?" "Maybe they settled out of court."

When we did go back out, the Judge announced that the alternate jurors would not be dismissed during our deliberations. Joe and Claudette and Murray and Obie would languish in the room just to the right of the jury box, where we had occasionally glimpsed a mysterious refrigerator (not an item of evidence). They were still not to discuss the case!

"The hour is one-twenty," said His Honor, "and luncheon has been promised for one-thirty. Perhaps it would be well for you to go in and relax, and then at one-thirty lunch will be delivered, and you may proceed after lunch with your deliberations. Thank you."

"Mr. Fox, Would You Rise, Please?"

Finally.

We filed out as usual from the crowded, quiet court-room. Past His Honor and the defendants, who were probably studying our faces, our strides, maybe even our knuckles. I didn't think about the tremendous vibrations we must have been emanating there. My mind was not racing with large American thoughts (later for those); part of my head registered the fact that I was hungry again.

Finally; into that charmless jury room, with our luggage lined up on the floor along the walls, with rain streaming down the two windows. Our sandwiches still hadn't arrived. Mr. Wallace locked us in. Now we could really *talk*, but even that didn't seem to excite anybody; we still didn't know what strife and strain might be brewing. Nils said, "Shall we start?" Someone said, "The Judge said we should eat first." I said, "The hell with it. I think we should begin." Nobody disagreed.

But then there was a knock on our door. Mr. Wallace unlocked it from outside and stepped in. "Stop talking, please." Some men brought our lunch in bags within bags, and withdrew. We sorted out the packages and containers; Beiser of course didn't get his beer. We arranged ourselves at the table—not big enough for twelve people to sit at it comfortably, but we were able to manage our sandwiches. There was another knock, just as we were asking where the coffee was. The men brought in a large institutional urn, to our cheers, and set it on the window sill with milk and sugar and styrofoam cups. Then they left; again the sound of a key turning in the lock amused and alarmed me.

Ingram Fox, at the head of the table, facing Steve at the other end, started off with polite introductory remarks. Ingram speaks with baroque eloquence much of the time, but he began simply, by saying that we were a fine group who had become friends, who could reason together. There were several comments of agreement— grace notes to establish a tone of calm and geniality. I suggested that we might expedite our job by having a secret ballot; I had read somewhere that this is often a good idea. But nobody took to it. Instead, we agreed to make a preliminary round of brief opinions.

At Ingram's left, good old businesslike Charlie Bowser started off—said it seemed to him that the DA had presented a network of allegations that didn't hold together. Hiram Irizarry, assuring us that he would try to speak his English clearly, said much the same. Around it went, everyone speaking with a degree of formality. Nils, with his careful enunciation and slight Danish-English accent: "I think the conspiracy evidence is flimsy, but the problem of the oatmeal and the shoot-out near the red car ought to be discussed." This did start a discussion, but Steve said, "Let's not go into those things yet—let's go around the table first." Fine, fine. Bill Beiser said he thought there wasn't much to the conspiracy; I felt especially relieved to hear this from *him*. Then Steve: "The problem is whether there was a conspiracy. I think the likelihood of it seems weak. I believe White's and Roberts's stories, and I think there is a probability that a crime was committed, but I don't think there's enough proof for a conviction."

Gary, squeezed at a corner of the table between Steve and Ben Giles, talked about the grand jury's indictments, which he thought seemed too heavy for those defendants—"One of them could have been my son, though I don't know them." The defense seemed to have torn down the accusations, Gary said, but he hadn't completely decided on his verdict yet. I think most of us were playing it cool until we knew where everybody stood. Ben Giles, though, was forthright; he reminded us of the time when McKinney had asked White, defendant by defendant, whether he had ever heard them agree to kill anyone, and White had said no at each name. "Phillips hasn't proved anything," said Ben.

My way of playing it cagey was to say, "I don't feel that there is any case for the conspiracy charges, and I think that White pretty effectively undermined his own testimony, and that's as much as I'd want to say at this stage."

Then, at my left, the exuberant unknown quantity

Jim Butters: "To me, one thing points to a conspiracy. I believe the story of the oatmeal." But Butters, like many a citizen, can hold contradictory ideas in his head at the same time. He mentioned his doubts about a detail in the story of Kuwasi and Sekou, who presumably had opened the trunk of the red Dodge Dart with the car keys before they were surprised and ran off; and yet another cop told us he was able to start the red car's motor right away to drive it to the police station—which must have meant that he found keys in the ignition lock.

Fred Hills held some notes; he'd been jotting things down in the jury box that morning and the day before as the Judge summarized and charged us, none of us knowing that we would get verdict sheets to go by. He also, like the rest of us, hadn't known that the battery of charges would get pared down to twelve.

Fred's notes were well prepared and well said. "I don't feel that the District Attorney has proved his charges. He has an enormous burden to prove the case, and he just doesn't seem to have done it."

Then, Miss Yanes: "Well, one of the things that bothered me was the shoot-out." This gave me a scare; but she went on. "I don't see how the two men would fail to hit a cop at such short range, and still be expected to fire across the Harlem River. . . . And—now, I don't know anything about how strong blasting caps are supposed to be, but I wonder how one of them could cause that much damage at the Forty-fourth Precinct, especially if it was packed in with five sticks of clay and oatmeal." She said she hoped one of us could explain it to her. But nobody did.

Then Fox: "It's collusion by police. The Judge told us that conspiracy is like a play, in which all the players are responsible. In this case, the police wrote the prologue: the playwright has the upper hand, and he controls the characters. We heard contradiction after contradiction that turned out to be lies. How do I know the policemen didn't want to set a trap? The infiltrators were aiding and abetting. . . ."

So each of us had spoken, and nobody seemed to be hot for a guilty verdict. It was about 3:00 P.M.

Then a small jolt. Steve says there is one point he wants to discuss: the defections of Michael Tabor and Richard Moore. Steve doesn't want to find any verdict on them, he feels he doesn't want to pass judgment in absentia. He wants to "hang" on those two men. Butters agrees, and I begin to wonder whether shrewd Steve has brought the matter up because Butters has already hinted his own view of the matter; shrewd subtle Steve, perhaps giving Butters a chance to air the dissident opinion, with at least one agreeable listener to keep him from hardening his opposition.

Butters: "I don't think we should judge them if they aren't here."

Steve: "I don't want to find them guilty *or* innocent." After some protests from others, he says to the majority, "Would you want to find Moore and Tabor *guilty*, if you found the others guilty?" "Sure," says Bowser, with nods or echoes from the rest of us.

The empty sandwich wrappers were scattered

around the table; I had finished a sweet roll with coffee. We kept walking over to the big urn for refills. The two large casement windows, with their small panes, looked out on the dim May day. Trees in the park below had new spring leaves, but rain made the little square look desolate.

Ingram Fox had delegated to Steve the mechanics of our deliberations; a wise move, for Steve was gently helping to expedite our job. He held the thirteen verdict sheets—one two-page list for each defendant, enumerating the same twelve charges. He said, "Look—let's shelve this in absentia question for a moment and get the other points settled. I'll read the counts and we'll go around the table for a vote."

Steve read count number one: "The crime of conspiracy in the first degree . . ."

Bowser started: "Not guilty." Hiram: "Not guilty." Nils, Beiser, Steve, Gary, Giles, me, Butters, Fred, Nina Yanes, and Ingram—all "Not guilty." Yes, even Butters. Then Steve carefully read number two, and we went around. We were all quiet, sipping coffee; nobody was yelling Yippee. The rain poured. Steve went on with the other counts, and everyone said, "Not guilty." I began to feel that more light was streaming through the windows than the sun himself could have provided.

On count thirteen, possession of dangerous instruments and appliances on January 17—"Not guilty" all around. On the final charge, fifteen, possession of dangerous instruments on April 2, we had some discussion. Did Collier possess "pipe bombs," as the DA had called

them? What about the red-labeled can of gunpowder
that the police said was in Collier's bathroom? Fred read
from his notes—a neat speech including his opinion that
the police had to make up the gunpowder-can story in
order to go into the bathroom. (They had said that Collier handed them the can, which would have given them
the right to go in there in the absence of a search warrant.) Some of us, including me, said that even if Collier did have the gunpowder, he wasn't necessarily guilty.
Also, the pulled-apart shotgun shells that were said to
have been in the Shakurs' possession weren't useful
evidence.

"It was the way they were teaching each other,"
Bowser said.

Ingram: "You're assuming they *had* those things."

Bowser: "They could have had them, for a revolution class."

Fred: "Or they may have assembled some explosives just to be ready."

Beiser: "I find that plausible."

So we all seemed to be in accord. Steve said, "I
don't feel the least bit sorry for those guys. They weren't
all exactly Sunday-school teachers. And if you talk the
way they did, you have to expect that the police will go
out and try to pick you up."

Nobody mentioned guns.

So we went through the last count, twelve more
Not Guiltys. By 3:30 they were all taken care of, and
there remained only the matter of the two jurors who
wanted to "hang" on Tabor and Moore.

I went to the bathroom. Fred was saying that it would be dramatic and significant to walk out now with eleven acquittals, but that the Judge would surely not accept a hung verdict on the other two at that point; we could sit for three or four days trying to resolve the problem.

Inside the bathroom I couldn't make out the vociferous discussion very well, but during a lull I heard Steve say, "I'm weakening, Butters." Hiram came in. He said, "Well—hasn't taken very long so far." I said, "It's a great day, Hiram."

When we came back out they were still talking. I suppose it was Steve who suggested that we pass around the verdict sheets for the eleven defendants we had agreed on—we had to write "Not guilty" for each of the twelve counts. I forget which one I filled out, and I don't know which of us didn't get one.

Steve gathered those up when we were finished; he still had the sheets for Tabor and Moore. He slid one of them—Richard Moore—over to Butters, both sets still with the righthand column blank.

I stood up, walked over to the coffee urn, filled a cup; paced back and forth. I asked Miss Yanes if she wanted some coffee; no. Someone else, Gary maybe, got up and paced. At the table they raised their voices a little, talking across each other. Steve said once more, "I'm weakening, Butters."

Although I was restless, I already felt a hint of relief, the ebb, along with a faint undersurge of exaltation. I would have liked to clap my hands out the window to the rainy street thirteen stories below, or dance. But that funny argument went on.

Was there any way to loosen up this hassle, bring a happy end to it? Did I detect impatient sounds among the majority, anger that might antagonize our minority? I went to the table, stood behind my chair, broke in awkwardly and harshly over the chattering. "*I'd* like to say something!" Trying to subdue my voice: "I think we all should consider that these guys might have a valid point. They're agreed with us on all the other counts, they aren't unreasonable. I would suggest that we open our minds to the possibility of going along with them on this question. If we just consider it . . . maybe after thinking about it we still wouldn't change our minds. *I* might not. But I think it's worth considering."

Nobody expressed any disagreement.

I doubt if my intervention precipitated Butters's change of mind. I didn't listen closely to the argument as it went on, and I didn't notice when it stopped. After I paced a little more I looked down at the table and saw that Butters was writing "Not guilty" in the blanks on Moore's list, and Steve was doing the same on Tabor's.

Done.

Steve got up to summon the Court officer. "Wait a minute," someone said. "We were going to write down our addresses so we could keep in touch with each other." Steve said, "That's okay, it's going to take them a while to round up everybody—they've all left the courtroom." It was about 4:00.

Steve knocked on the door. We heard the key

turning outside, and Mr. Wallace stepped in. "Stop deliberating, please."

"We have," says Steve. "We've got a verdict."

Mr. Wallace, expressionless, locked us in again and we began to chat, to write our addresses down; it was Steve, of course, who would make them up into a list and send a copy to each of us. I reminded my friends that they were welcome to come to my apartment for a drink as soon as we were released.

Hiram and I had playfully told the alternates that we would try to signal the verdict through the bathroom wall (I forget what the code was). We pounded, but it didn't work.

We all relaxed and went on yammering. At about 4:30 we heard a knock, the door was opened, and we filed into the courtroom for the last time. Deadpan, except that Fred attempted a small smile toward the defendants. All the black faces at the defendants' table; intent black and white faces in the spectator section.

I was stunned to see that the usual contingent of guards, a dozen or so sitting behind the defendants, was now a standing wall of blue. Bristling. There were many more men, shielding us from the spectators. (I heard later that there had been another roomful of policemen nearby, in case they had been needed to contain Armageddon; and I read that dinner had been planned for us across the street with sixty-four guards in attendance.) It made me feel terribly important. Having stared at them, I turned my eyes again to the Panthers and their lawyers; we knew something they didn't know.

The four alternates had come out of their room and were sitting down low, at the right of the jury box, hidden by us from the spectators. I swung my arm behind Steve's chair and tried to signal okay to Claudette, but she didn't notice.

The court clerk says, "Mr. Fox, would you rise, please?"

Ingram stands up, holding the verdict sheets.

"Members of the jury, have you reached a verdict?"

"Yes," says Ingram. This time it *is* like the movies.

The clerk says, "As to the defendant Lumumba Shakur, on the first count charging the crime of conspiracy in the first degree, how do you find, sir, guilty, or not guilty?"

"Not guilty," says Ingram, and there is a stir in the great room.

As the clerk continues, Ingram holds the verdict sheets down at his waistline—no need to refer to them. The import of this slowly floods the room.

From the transcript:

"As to the second count, charging attempt to commit the crime of murder, how do you find, sir?"

"Not guilty."

"The third count, the charge of an attempt to commit the crime of murder, how do you find, sir?"

"Not guilty."

"As to the fourth count, charging attempt to commit the crime of murder, how do you find, sir?"

"Not guilty."

"As to the fifth count, the charge of an attempt to commit the crime of murder, how do you find?"

"Not guilty."

"As to the sixth count, the charge of conspiracy in the second degree, how do you find, sir?"

"Not guilty."

"As to the seventh count, the charge of an attempt to commit the crime of arson in the first degree, how do you find, sir?"

"Not guilty."

"As to the eighth count, charging the crime of arson in the first degree, how do you find, sir?"

"Not guilty."

"As to the ninth count, charging the crime of arson in the second degree, how do you find, sir?"

"Not guilty."

"As to the tenth count, charging the crime of conspiracy in the third degree, how do you find, sir?"

"Not guilty."

"As to the thirteenth count, charging the crime of possession of weapons and dangerous instruments and appliances, how do you find, sir?"

"Not guilty."

"As to the fifteenth count, charging the crime of possession of weapons and dangerous instruments and appliances, how do you find, sir?"

"Not guilty."

Boom. Lumumba is free. Afeni gives a loud sobbing cry, throws her head on his shoulder; his arm goes around her. She continues to weep—sometimes turns her wet face to us. The spectators are joyfully agitated.

Next comes the same litany of charges for Richard Moore, one of the defectors. Ingram has twelve more sets of twelve to go—talk about playing the dozens! Not guilty. Not guilty. Counselor Crain swings around in his chair to embrace Ali Bey Hassan across the table. There may be tears in Counselor Bloom's eyes, as in mine. Counselor Lefcourt puts his hands to his Afro hair and grins and shakes his head. This time, as my eyes meet those of the lawyers, we can smile at each other.

The two prosecutors, sitting near us, stare down at their table, like statues entitled Dismay. The Judge is impassive and no doubt tremendously . . . interested. I look over at the spectators—can't see all of them past the wall of guards. A young white woman at the reporters' table is smiling at me. I try to see Murray Kempton's thoughts and emotions and paragraphs. The waves of import are almost too potent; I have to sink my face into my hands a couple of times and breathe through my mouth. Then I start exulting with Fred, and Steve mutters, "Cool it, cool it," which seems a good idea for the moment.

Ingram finishes his 156th Not Guilty.

The clerk has a few more ritual pronouncements, words in a quaint dead language: "Members of the jury, hearken unto your verdicts as they stand recorded, you say you find each of the defendants not guilty of all the charges brought against them, and so say you all."

Judge Murtagh says, "Mr. Fox, ladies and gentle-

men of the jury, once again I wish to thank you sincerely for your dedicated service. You have served as jurors
in the best tradition of our law. The community is grateful to you for your patience in enduring a long trial
over many months and furnishing genuine service to the
administration of justice. You are discharged with the
sincere thanks of the Court."

Thereupon: shouting and clapping. As we walked
out, past the defendants, I return their power salute. The
tornado of joy follows us into the jury room. We
are talking and laughing as we pick up our suitcases
and walk to our special elevator.

I hardly remember riding down; I remember that
my mouth was painfully dry.

Amazement All Around

Some of the jurors stayed for a while in the main-floor lobby of the courthouse, among reporters and television cameramen and lawyers and defendants. Amazing to think that our two-and-a-half-hour deliberation dissolved those two-year bonds, bars, constraints., Besides Afeni, Joan Bird and Lee Roper walked out, with Alex McKeiver, Walter Johnson, Clark Squire, and Curtis Powell. The other defendants were held because other charges hung over them.

Since I didn't feel like talking to reporters, I scurried home. Soon about half a dozen of the jurors showed up. We had a couple of drinks and tried to unwind; Joe Rainato telephoned to say that the defense lawyers were giving a party at their commune office, on Bleecker Street, so we took the fifteen-minute walk, in the rain, to the beat-up old building, rode the shaky elevator to the fifth floor, where we were greeted by hugs and kisses from women, ferocious warm handshakes and embraces from the men—many people I didn't recognize, although they had been at the trial regularly and knew the juror's faces well.

I did recognize the defendants—amazing to encounter them now, across a gulf that had been bridged but was still a gulf. Amazing to shake hands and talk with the lawyers and their wives, to meet Ruth Silber, one of the lawyers' most stalwart and enthusiastic assistants, who had a lot to say about how wonderful everyone was. We drank champagne and nibbled at potato chips or something; it was a happy blur to me then and still is.

My foremost thought about the trial was, How did the grand juries decide to bring those heavy indictments? There is something wrong with the way those august bodies are constituted. They are mainly the fat cats of the community, who, like most of us comfortable folks, have not heeded Martin Duberman's advice to be in touch "with the felt experience of others"—the poor, the disaffected, the angry underdogs—to have some conception of their lives, their feelings, their language. If they were in touch, they would ask a lot of hard questions, would make the DAs work harder for their indictments. As it is now, grand juries at the very least can be manipulated, evidently, to frighten people with that "chilling effect" that is the death of freedom. It's expensive, too. According to the newspapers, the State of New York spent $2 million on the case in the two years between arrests and acquittals. Several trials since then—especially the Berrigan "conspiracy" with its hung jury and Angela Davis's acquittal by plain sensible jurors like us—have kept me thinking about it, have kept me worrying.

In the weeks after the trial I met several times with jurors and lawyers in various combinations—a couple of times with Lumumba Shakur and Curtis Powell and Afeni, just for brief good wishes. Some of the jurors talked about the trial on radio and television. When we got together once or twice with Jackie Freidrich, who had reported the trial for the *East Village Other*, and Margo Adler, who had reported it for WBAI radio, we went over all the funny and absurd and heavy things we hadn't been able to talk about, with great elation and camaraderie. The elation subsided; the camaraderie has of course tapered off, but it seems to be there to stay.

I learned that Afeni was living at an apartment only a couple of blocks from mine. I saw her maybe six or eight times in the year that followed. She brought the baby (born in June, a month after the acquittal) to my office, with Joan Bird, and I took them to lunch; the baby, Tupa (a.k.a. Parrish), was extraordinarily well-behaved, though when I asked Afeni if he was always like that she said, "No—he's a baby!"

One day Afeni brought a couple of friends to my apartment—Frankie Zith and his wife Dee. Joe Rainato came also, and some of my friends. We talked about the long voir dire.

"All we wanted," Afeni said, "was a jury with a conscience."

Dee said, "And you got one with soul."